Religion and Education: Framing and Mapping a Field

Religion and Education

Volumes published in this Brill Research Perspectives title are listed at *brill.com/rpre*

Religion and Education:
Framing and Mapping a Field

By

Stephen G. Parker
Jenny Berglund
David Lewin
Deirdre Raftery

BRILL

LEIDEN | BOSTON

This paperback book edition is simultaneously published as issue 1.1 (2019) of *Religion and Education*, DOI:10.1163/25895303-12340001.

Library of Congress Control Number: 2019910384

Typeface for the Latin, Greek, and Cyrillic scripts: "Brill". See and download: brill.com/brill-typeface.

ISBN 978-90-04-41294-1 (paperback)
ISBN 978-90-04-41295-8 (e-book)

Printed by Printforce, the Netherlands

Contents

Religion and Education: Framing and Mapping a Field

Stephen G. Parker
University of Worcester, UK
s.parker@worc.ac.uk

Jenny Berglund
Stockholm University, Sweden
jenny.berglund@hsd.su.se

David Lewin
University of Strathclyde, UK
david.lewin@strath.ac.uk

Deirdre Raftery
University College Dublin, Ireland
deirdre.raftery@ucd.ie

Abstract

This publication makes the case for 'religion and education' as a distinct, but cross-disciplinary, field of inquiry. To begin with, consideration is given to the changing dynamic between 'religion and education' historically, and the differing understandings of religious education within it. Next, 'religion and education' is examined from methodologically specific perspectives, namely the philosophical, historical and sociological. The authors outline the particular insights to be gleaned about 'religion and education' on the basis of their commitment to these methodological standpoints. Overall, this publication is concerned with demonstrating the scope of the field, and the importance of having a range of disciplinary, and interdisciplinary, perspectives informing it.

Keywords

religion – education – religious education – public sphere – methodology – cross-disciplinary – interdisciplinary

Introduction: Religion and Education
An Overview

Stephen G. Parker

This inaugural issue of the Brill Research Perspectives on Religion and Education (hereafter *Religion and Education*) is devoted to mapping the field of 'religion and education' (hereafter R&E). As editor-in-chief, I am very pleased to be able to launch this series at a time when the significance of R&E is strongly to the fore, and its importance as a focus for scholarship as an aspect of religion in the public sphere is widely recognized. Working with my associate editors, who bring their distinctive expertise to the project (Jenny Berglund, (sociology), Leslie J. Francis (psychology), David Lewin (philosophy), and Deirdre Raftery (history)) we intend that this new journal will provide the opportunity to focus upon themes and debates in current research on the intersecting areas of R&E from a variety of disciplinary and international perspectives. In this vein, we welcome proposals for future issues from scholars from all parts of the world on topics of relevance to the journal's broad remit, and from differing methodological standpoints. The long-form format of this journal makes the publication of in-depth studies uniquely possible. It is my hope that such in-depth studies from a diversity of national contexts will ultimately provide a base of knowledge for a more substantive perspective on R&E which is both informative of the research agenda, but which also makes possible a basis for comparison of scholarly trends and issues of policy and practice globally.

1   Religion and Education: Beyond Curricula and Schooling, Multi-contextual, International and Interdisciplinary Perspectives

R&E is here understood in a broad and most expansive way, along the lines delineated by Anna Strhan (undated) in a virtual special issue of the *Journal of Philosophy of Education* and discussed in more detail below. Thus, R&E includes studies on religious upbringing, religious education (and its various namesakes as a subject) and the curriculum, matters related to faith-based schooling, issues of religious identity, and the religious ideas of education. In the *Religion and Education* we are, therefore, concerned to ensure that the journal is not restricted to schooling-related matters and that it gives coverage to research on aspects of R&E in the domestic, familial, cultural and institutional contexts of religion, whether that be, for example, child-rearing practice, the Madrasa and similar environments, such as Sunday schools, or aspects of devotional and religious life which are in the broadest sense educational. Equally, we want the *Religion and Education* to be concerned with within-religion educational issues and questions of life-long learning, for instance adult theological education, or learning in other faith-based educational contexts. Additionally, this journal's remit is intended to encompass broader matters of R&E, in politics and society: questions of church/religion and the state, legal and ethical questions in R&E, and the part that religion might play in social cohesion through educational systems and programmes, which are aimed at shaping the public understanding of religion. Matters of R&E have public and political consequences, many of which are topical, such as the rights of parents to educate their children in the religion of the home, to questions of faith schooling and the nature and function of religious education in schools. Thus, R&E is not only a matter for those who deem themselves to be religious, it is a political and legal matter of relevance to all of us regardless of our (non-) religious perspective or persuasion. Significantly, this journal is committed to historicizing R&E as well as encouraging the publication of studies which approach matters in R&E from a contemporary point of view.

Moreover, as this first issue will make clear, the intersection between R&E is multi-contextual and international. This intersection occurs in specific and contrasting macro-, meso- and micro-contexts, which have unique elements and domain specific issues and questions. For instance, at a national level studying R&E as an issue in one nation will, of course, have to deal with a different set of contingencies in another. Matters of R&E in Northern Ireland, for instance, will be different and distinct than those in, for example, France. Similarly, questions of R&E in one faith-based context will differ from another, and one domestic cultural context to another. There are historical, political, social and cultural contingencies, which make the contexts of R&E diverse, requiring methodological sensitivity and plurality. Additionally, from a methodological perspective account needs to be taken of the dynamics of religious change always experienced across societies, not least in the present with the rising number of people self-identifying as spiritual or 'non-religious' (Lee, 2017), as well as the continuing vibrancy of new religious movements and fundamentalisms (Chryssides and Zeller, 2016). The study of these and other cultural phenomena has implications for the study of R&E.

Likewise, we intend that the *Religion and Education* be cross-disciplinary in content. Bringing together under one umbrella contrasting methodological perspectives in an overt way unique in the field. In doing so we hope to generate interdisciplinary perspectives, insights and connections which fuel further questions and research.

Such an expansive take on R&E has rarely been delineated in this way in the academy, and we believe it to be unique amongst academic journals. This may well be because of aspects of R&E tend to be dealt with in disciplinary, curriculum, cultural or national silos. This journal aims at breaking out of this tendency, towards developing a more expansive, and at the same time more nuanced, picture on the subject-matter. We believe the time is ripe to take a broader and deeper perspective on R&E matters, whilst demonstrating the lengthy historical and sometimes interconnected nature of these issues.

In section one, I begin to elaborate upon how R&E might be usefully framed to augment our knowledge of the field internationally and multi-methodologically. I argue that though religious education in schools is a crucial dimension of R&E, it should not equate with it. Additionally, I point out that religious education may be conceptualised in differing ways, and that sometimes ideas about religious education become conflated when discussing them in scholarly and professional circles, leading to a good deal of confusion. The section concludes by arguing that studies of religious education would benefit by paying closer attention to research in Religious Studies, and R&E would benefit from the international and interdisciplinary perspectives that this journal stands for.

In section two, Deirdre Raftery focuses upon examining the relationship between Christian missions and the history of R&E. She points out that thus far the historiography is denominationally skewed, towards the contribution of the Protestant missions to education. This important observation draws attention to the wider point that historical perspectives on R&E need to take account of denominational- and religion-specific differences and contributions.

In section three, David Lewin presents a philosophical perspective upon R&E, unpicking how each term has been conceptualised and understood. His basic argument being that the way in which religion has been constructed within educational debates has led to a somewhat distorted impression of what the educational issues are. Likewise, how education has been framed.

In section four, Jenny Bergland looks at different schools of sociology and their founders. From there she asks how sociology might inform perspectives on schooling, not least in religious education, focusing upon an examination of the methods which might be deployed to understand the social contexts of the school and classroom. The experiences of students in Islamic educational contexts, and the influences of various media on understandings of religion, are provided as instances which might be informed by using the sociological methodologies and methods.

I conclude this issue by moving on to discuss some under-developed research themes in R&E and religious education, related to historicizing, contextualising and conceptualising; the spatial, material and the sensory; mission, empire and nation building; and the agency of children. In doing so, I recommend agenda for further research in R&E and related cross-disciplinary fields. Next, I examine the problematic and uncertain relationship between, on the one hand, religious education and on the other theological and religious studies. Finally, I discus the potential ways in which this journal might contribute to encouraging further thinking in the critical important field of R&E.

Religion and Education: Framing and Mapping the Field

Stephen G. Parker

This introductory section sets out to make the case for R&E as a field of inquiry, in and of itself. It makes the case that research in of R&E (and religious education) benefit from being both contextualised and historicized. Specifically, the section explores the dynamic relationship between R&E in the modern and contemporary periods, particularly with the advent of the nation-state, and state-provided education systems, which in many societies have developed to provide a secular form schooling (often alongside separate religious schools). Secondly, the section examines the place of religious education within R&E, focusing upon the variety of conceptualizations of religious education, based as they are upon differing theoretical and/or theological presuppositions, the changing social purposes of religious education, and the contrasting social practices and understandings of research in religious education, and education more generally (Afdal, 2008).

1   Religion and Education in the Public Sphere

Rarely do studies of R&E (or religious education) historicize matters, or contextualise them in particular national histories (aside from a few notable exceptions e.g. Osmer. and Schweitzer, 2003, Braaten, 2015). One of the early attempts to do so was Robert Ulich's 1968 book, a *History of Religious Education*. In this, Ulich starkly points out that 'all early education was religious, and all early religion was also educational'; that the priests of the religions were once the teachers; and that it was only when the state began to intervene that elements of schooling became secularized (Ulich, 1968: v). R&E in the past were virtually synonymous. This early relationship between R&E may be quite straightforwardly depicted as in figure 1, where the educational is embedded within the religious, and forms a significant proportion of the activities of the religious life. For instance, the liturgy, rituals and rites of passage of religion may be seen as religiously educative, inducting people into religion; acting as an aide memoire of the foundational stories of religion; providing opportunity to rehearse and recommit to the moral, spiritual and vocational purposes of the faith.

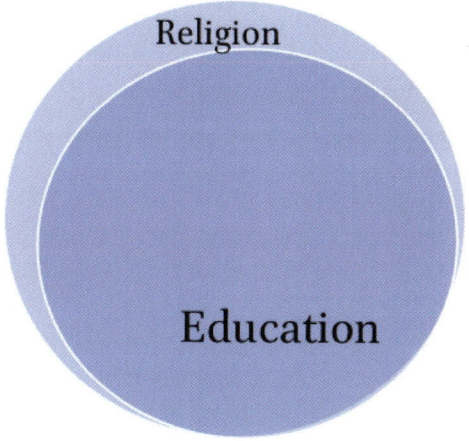

FIGURE 1
Religion and education are virtually
synonymous

With the advent of a public-school system in many modern societies, even in those which organised to have religious schooling alongside a state-funded system, the specifically religious (or confessional) became a more marginal, indeed problematic, purpose of schooling. Moreover, the aims of religious education in such contexts have tended to be revised, in response to the religiously diverse and secular constituencies public-school systems serve. Formation in this context, as depicted by figure 2, is envisaged as being for secular rather than religious ends. Even for some religious adherents, the separation of schooling from its purely religious ends was desirable as a way of ensuring that minority religious identities were protected from religious proselytization (e.g. some English Nonconformists argued on this basis for secular education to avoid their children being forced to receive the teachings of the Church of England (Parker and Freathy, 2020)).

Despite the secularization of schooling to which Ulich points, broader and informal forms of education remain religion's well-spring. Indeed, a religion's very survival depends upon the transmission of its teachings to children and young people, or conversions to it. Even if the social dynamics of these processes—whether that be socialization in the home, through forms of catechesis, or through religious schooling and religious curricula—these also have the potential to become sites of resistance and religious transformation, as Susan Ridgely and Rachael Shillitoe have both potently noted (see for example Ridgely 2011; Shillitoe, forthcoming). One might also observe that within the dynamics of R&E, religions not only self-perpetuate, they also change. It is within the interplay of knowledge (revelation), learning (ritual) and the agency of the adherent (discipleship and devotion), that religions are lived, defined and even at times reformed.

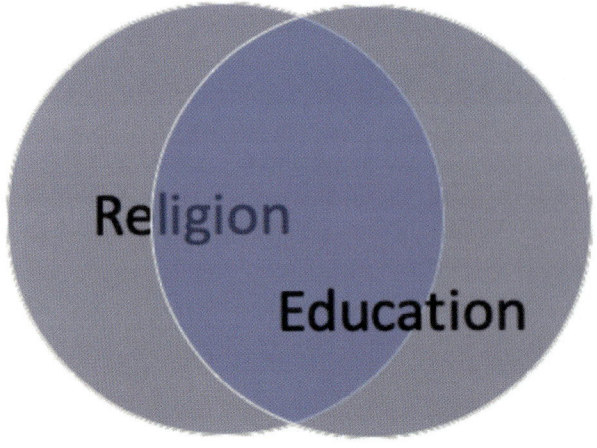

FIGURE 2
Education as an activity
emerges as distinct from
religion

However, from the late eighteenth century, as Jurgen Habermas (2015) argued, a distinct public sphere emerged, and along with it many facets of social and political organisation, including state-provided education systems. This growing public sphere, and the wider social and educational dynamics of modernity, served to complicate the relationship between religion and education as a domestic and religious institutional matter, in a variety of ways, in that religious education in some places became a function of state-provided schooling rather than an activity of religions alone. Consequently, as the public has become increasingly divorced from the private sphere, a more complicated relationship between R&E emerged, which may be depicted as in figure 3.

Much could be said about the ways in which the dynamic inter-relationship between religion, education, and the public and private spheres has played out historically on questions, for example, around the nature and purpose of religious education, and what it is permissible to teach in schools. These questions continue to be a matter of public debate, but they have long historical lineages. To what extent can religious purposes be served, if at all, by such religious education has had to be qualified and reframed because of the necessity of having wider public-sphere oriented goals for the subject. In some contexts, negotiation over the aims of religious education is ongoing. Additionally, any operative model of Church-State relationship needed to be reformulated as a result of dynamics and demands of wider society, as well as having a public education system. Indeed, we can see this kind of reformulation happening over time in many of the nations of Europe where traditionally Church and State had strong bonds. Likewise, the existence and purpose of so-called 'faith schools' (or schools with a religious foundation, or with confessional

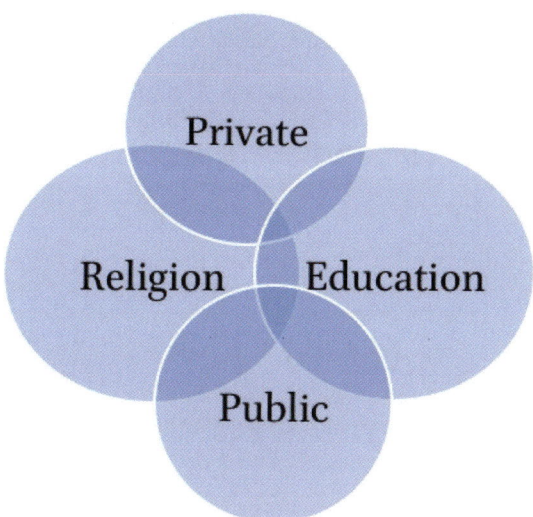

FIGURE 3
Religion and education in
societies with a public sphere,
in which the private connotes
the domestic and religious
institutional contexts

purposes) in such societies is consistently called into question, their purposes
having to be framed differently, stressing for example the ways in which such
schools provide a service for society, not just for children of believing families
(Church of England, 2016).

Moreover, the balance and dynamics between the four elements of the relationship between religion, education and the private and public spheres may
differ from society to society, and indeed within particular societies, as Damon
Mayrl (2015) has demonstrated of the United States and Australia. These dynamics, as Mayrl observes, create varying levels of secularity within the organisational structures and types of schools across national education systems,
depending upon how national education systems came to be. Secularity, expressed through the development of schooling, is a political project and occurs
at differing rates across societies (Mayrl, 2016, p.26). Here we see how historical contingencies and political and cultural realities across societies mould
and shape matters of religion and education. Within this dynamic, theologies
and theories of Church/religion-state relations play their part in defining the
relationship between the domains (Buchardt, 2015). Presently, there is much
debate around the relative weight of religious perspectives and influences, as
well as secular ones, over matters of R&E, typified by Liam Gearon and Joseph
Prud'homme's recent book *State Religious Education and the State of Religious
Life* (2018). Gearon and Prud'homme provide a robust argument for religious
perspectives in education, and for the important educative function of bibli-
cal instruction as cultural education, especially in societies founded upon the
Bible, or having predominantly Protestant cultural histories.

Debates over the place of religion in education are perennial. In the present, such debates appear to be particularly acute, perhaps due to the creation of more religiously plural societies, as well as a growing secular presence in many national contexts. Such debates are potentially better understood if framed using the proposed heuristic above, that is in the wider context of the formation (and reformulation) of a public sphere and within this the development of a public education system. It is curious, however, that researchers have only rarely considered these historical and political contingencies as relevant when debating matters of religion and education (see Osmer and Schweitzer, 2003), choosing instead to focus predominantly on debating the ideas which have shaped religious educational practises (see for example, Jackson, 2015; Gearon, 2018; Jackson, 2018).

I would hope that this new journal will provide opportunities to examine both the larger matters which impact and shape R&E, and the narrower ones, focused upon the history and influence of particular ideas upon religious education, in greater depth and from differing methodological perspectives.

2   The History of Religion and Education as a Field of Inquiry

One might date the beginning of R&E as a distinct field of inquiry to the point from which the systematic study of it began, that is to the history of knowledge of its various constituent disciplinary elements in the academy. One way of mapping the recent history of R&E as a field is by an examination of the published literature encompassing it, the study of which could be very fruitful in identifying a range of things, including the scholarly priorities at any given point in time (Freathy et al., 2014).

An early, if not the earliest, R&E journal, was that of the Religious Education Association of the United States (founded in 1903), namely *Religious Education* (Kathan, 2013). First published in 1906, this predominantly Protestant Christian journal's early issues were peppered with articles about the organisation of Christian religious education internationally, the nature of Sunday schooling, and children's moral and spiritual instruction. Interestingly, as early as the first issues of this journal, psychological insights were being drawn upon to inform approaches to religious education. Somewhat later, in the British context, the journal *Religion and Education*, first published in 1934, also became a vehicle for the discussion and dissemination of ideas around Christian education, the relationship to the broader Christian mission, the kinds of organisational bodies and networks which might enable Christian religious education to happen, and how religious education in schools might be effectively taught (Parker, Freathy and Doney, 2016). Predominantly then, these early journals of R&E were concerned to build insights into the effective means by which religious education in schools, seen as an aspect of Christian mission within a society thought to be broadly Christian in nature, could and should be taught.

A further analysis, this time of the constitution of the journals' editorial boards, indicates something of the epistemological basis of the field, and the social and professional audience the periodicals sought to target. Thus, to begin with both the journals Religious Education and Religion in Education's editorial boards were made up of ministers of religion and head teachers. University-based academics were in the minority. One might conclude from this that the knowledge-base drawn upon to inform agenda then came from within religion and the disciplines of theology, and was only weakly in dialogue with practitioners and practice. The relationship between academia and schools, research and practice, was at this point in time at least, loose and unidirectional.

Systematic, social scientific methodologies only featured as normative in research practice in R&E from the 1980s, if the content of the journals cited here is anything to go by. The reasons for this are many, but almost certainly, in the British context, this was due to more of an identification of R&E with research in education than research in religion. Research in R&E from then onwards has tended to be mostly influenced by the theories and methodologies of the social sciences. One of the effects of the identification of research in R&E with the social scientific disciplines has been a relative disconnection between scholarship in R&E with scholarship in Theology and Religious Studies, of which more is said below.

A much closer analysis of the range of journals in the field of R&E over time (see the list of journals at the end of this issue) has the potential to offer many interesting insights. For instance, one might ask, which disciplinary methodologies are being drawn upon over time? Which theories and/or theological perspectives tend to dominate in particular periods? Who are the leading voices at any particular point in time? What is the balance of voices in terms of religion and denomination? How international is dialogue in the field? What are the long-term trends? Similarly, undertaking a textual or discourse or thematic analysis of the content, biographical and prosopographical analysis of authors, an analysis of their disciplinary backgrounds and published works cited, would identify scholarly preoccupations historically, within and across particular local and national jurisdictions.

A cursory reading of early issues of these journals reveals that over time the locus of research in R&E has shifted from the home and informal contexts of learning, such as the Sunday school (Archibald, 1926), to the study of learning in government-funded (or part-funded) school classrooms (e.g. Schweitzer and Boschki eds., 2018). This shift revealingly demonstrates how matters of R&E have become as much focused on putative secular contexts as well as the specifically religious. Moreover, religious education has found new mediations through radio, film, television and in the contemporary through digital technologies, though the implications of the latter have been barely explored (Parker, Crutchley and Roberts, 2020). Seemingly, matters of R&E have moved from being a private, within-religion, matter to its public and civic functions through the curriculum and schooling (Habermas 2015, Hannam, 2018).

3   Types of Religious Education

As indicated, religious education (policy, curriculum and pedagogy) is but one aspect of scholarship on R&E, albeit a highly significant one. However, what often goes unacknowledged in debates about religious education (variously called: Religious Instruction, Religious Studies, Religions Education) is that there are multiple understandings of the term. Below are six sometimes overlapping ways in which religious education has been, or is, conceptualized. Aspects of each of these are worthy of critical study, utilizing differing methodologies in doing so. It is notable that some of these concepts of religious education predominate more in specific national contexts, to do with the influence of national religious histories upon the styles of religious education which develop in the public-school system.

The following are attempts to delineate the operative types of religious education. No values judgement of these understandings is intended.

4   Religious Education as Nurture into the Religious Way of Life

As noted, religions depend upon forms of religious education for their continuation. In this category, religious education is understood to include religious socialization in the domestic context by the adoption of particular child-rearing practises (Hull, 1991; Browning and Miller-McLemore, 2009). Included in this understanding of religious education might be the catechumenate, a Sunday or Hebrew school, or madrasa, etc. These informal contexts, or programmes of learning within the life of a congregation, have the distinct end of inculcating into the religious way of life, with a view to children and young people become part of the religious community, sustaining their commitment. These forms of religious education are often directed towards supporting children through rites of initiation into the religion, and thus fostering religious experience of some kind. This form of religious education is often allied to the missionary expansion of the Church or religious community. It is closely aligned to the second form religious education described below, but in this instance it relates more to the domestic and institutional context than to the public one.

5   Religious Education as Practical Theology

Closely aligned to the above is the idea of religious education as a fundamental constituent of (Christian) practical theology in the tradition of Friedrich Schleiermacher (Schleiermacher, 2011). This form of religious education draws upon theology and the insights and methodologies of the social sciences in the service of Christian church (Roebben and Warren, 2001). It is a combined pastoral and educational understanding of religious education across the generations for the strengthening of the Christian community, its mission, and the support of Christian discipleship. This concept of religious education may extend beyond the Christian community *per se* to, for example, religious education in public schools, although in these instances the religious education is mostly taught in religious/denominational environments (Mercer and Miller-McLemore, 2005). In this way of conceptualising religious education there is also an element of the prophetic, that is of faith speaking to the issues of society of which religious and theological education is seen to play its part (Hull, 2014; Pirner et al, 2019). Insofar as other religions have distinct pastoral outlooks, religious education may be seen as a practical activity aligned to the purposes of fostering faith development and belonging to the religious tradition in question.

6   Religious Education as Nation Building

State education which has religious education (or a namesake) as a constituent part of the school curriculum, especially where the church (or religion) is closely aligned to the state, or is established, has led to religious education sometimes being understood and utilized as a means of nation building

(Parker, 2012; Gates, 2017; Parker and Freathy, 2017; Mayrl, 2018; Gearon and Prud'homme, 2018[1]). Moreover, as societies have become more religiously diverse, religious education has been deployed to play its part in fostering, what in British government rhetoric of the early 2000s was called 'community cohesion' (Grimmitt, 2010; Parker and Freathy, 2010). In this context, religious education is seen as part of a gamut of strategies by which migrant groups can be assimilated into a host culture, it being seen as a key aspect of citizenship formation.

7   Religious Education as Religious Literacy

More recently, religious education has been spoken of as being for the goal of the development of 'religious literacy', and a religious literate population (Francis and Dinham, 2016; Melloni and Caddedu, 2019). Recognizing the religiously plural (and non-religious) nature of most Western societies, discourse on religious literacy frames it as concerned with the attainment of necessary knowledge and understanding of religion in order to exercise the capacities of being a citizen. Religious education in school is seen as one of the means by which religious literacy can be fostered and developed, along with other work-based training programmes, or through religious broadcasting and other media.

8 ·   Religious Education as Intercultural/Interreligious Education

Similarly, religious education is sometimes viewed as a key aspect of the development of intercultural/interreligious learning and education (Nesbitt, 2004; Pirner (et al), 2018). Again, this way of framing religious education is as a tool by which mutual understanding between different social and religious groups can be attained, especially in religious plural societies. Seen as a form of multicultural education, grouped with language learning and citizenship formation as aspects of the educational process (*Bildung* or human development), religious education as intercultural/interreligious education has a political imperative to it, linked to freedom of religion and the protection of religious identity, and human rights (Council of Europe, 2005).

---

1   Gearon and Prud'homme write of the relationship between Christianity and nationhood in England, the US and Australia, but what of those of differing faiths?

9 Religious Education as Preparation for the Academic Study of Religion

As religious education has sought to attain equivalent standing as an academic subject in schools and, with the concomitant attainment of examination results, it has become increasingly aligned to its equivalent subject/s in universities, principally the disciplines of Theology and Religious Studies. In Britain, at least, developments in the school subject have paralleled (though not directly mimicked) those in universities. Thus, for instance, religious education rebranded itself as Religious Studies as the name for the examinable subject in schools the period after the 1980s. However, methodologically and pedagogically the subject has in this context become plural, the multiple and sometimes conflicting aims for the subject resulting in a number of different approaches to teaching of it (see Grimmitt, 2000). Recent pedagogies and approaches have sought to rationalize and legitimize this plurality in terms of preparing children and young people to study Theology and Religious Studies at university level, inculcating them into the approaches and methodologies utilized in higher education (Freathy et al, 2017).

10 Religious Education as an Idea

The fact of that there are operative, contrasting, and regularly blurred conceptualisations of 'religious education' goes some way to explaining why debates over the subject are often highly contested. Being clear about what one means by 'religious education' when one uses the term is quite obviously therefore important. Appreciating how one's own understanding of 'religious education' is being framed, and the premises upon which it is based, is important for dialogue amongst academics, and between academics, educationalists and other members of society. Moreover, even within educational systems which have different types of school, those with a religious foundation and those without for instance, understandings of 'religious education' may differ.

Similarly, from a historical and philosophical perspective, it is important to recognise that 'religious education' means different things at different points in time (as well as having contrasting meanings at the same time) (Freathy and Parker, 2010). Religious education has a past, and a political, cultural and religious context. Thus, religious education is ripe for historical, contextual study. Such studies have the potential to reveal its history as an idea having multiple influences, and one which is in flux, contrasting and changing across times and societies.

Where the lines between types of religious education in operation are un-clear, it follows that the aims and purposes are also likely to be obfuscated. In this journal we are interested in studies of all types of religious education and across religious traditions (notwithstanding the contested notion of religion itself, which for the sake of brevity I have not touched upon here). In practise how one is understanding the term religious education when using it is clearly important, and a critical consciousness of the different conceptualisations of the term will be encouraged editorially.

Themes and Approaches in Research on Religion in the History of Education: Missionaries, Monasteries, Methodologies

Deirdre Raftery

1 Introduction

A few years ago, I attended a history of education conference at which several delegates presented on research that either drew on sources from religious archives, or that interrogated connections between religions and the provision of schooling in the past. There were two moments at that conference that had a strong impact on me. One was during the question-and-answer session, following a paper on an aspect of the history of Christian Brothers' schools that analysed an aspect of their work in the education of working-class boys. An audience member later commented to the speaker that she could not understand why anyone would want to do research that valorised elements of Christian Brothers' education, given that members of the institute had been implicated in cases of child-abuse. The second event at that conference that struck me with force, was the audience reaction to a paper on convent education. Daily routines that were part of the legacy of nineteenth century convent life seemed ridiculous to some audience members. In the event, the speaker allowed a deeply serious religious context to become light entertainment, and the opportunity to lead a nuanced discussion of obsolete faith-related practices in education was lost.

Both of these moments reminded me that when religion, religious practices, and religious personae enter historical debate, there is endless scope for misunderstanding, bias, and even hostility. Historical research on R&E can be 'triggering': it can call up unwelcome memories and evoke emotions. Indeed, the involvement of religious in the provision of education is still a contested area today. But historical research in this area is necessary, and of immense value. Incisive scholarship on the history of incidents of clerical child abuse in education is very important; so too is research into ways in which religious organisations pioneered education for the poor. Nuanced discussions of how religious practices were transmitted through education in the past are needed; equally we need much more research on ways in which education was designed, delivered and controlled by religious institutes and denominational philanthropic groups. The use of theoretical perspectives in such inquiries, including the lenses of gender, race and ethnicity, will allow for a clearer understanding of a very complicated research area. Above all, balance in the historical narrative is crucial, if research on religion and our education past is to be valid and valuable.

Scholarship in which historians of education have researched religions and religious contexts, appeared in an article in a special issue of *History of Education* (Raftery, 2012), published to mark the fiftieth anniversary of that journal. To meet the editorial requirements of the special issue, the article was confined to the examination of research that had been published in the fifty-year life of *History of Education*. This article allows me to expand the discussion, to include work that has been published in monographs, edited books, and in many journals, including the *Women's History Review, Religions, Paedagogica Historica, Gender and Education*, the *Canadian Catholic Historical Association Historical Studies, Women's Studies International Forum, American Catholic Studies, International Studies in Catholic Education*, the *Journal of Research on Christian Education, Gender and Society*, the *Oxford Review of Education*, the *Asian Journal of Social Science*, the *Journal of Women's History, Journal of the Australian Catholic Historical Society* and *Irish Educational Studies*. While the broad scope of some of this article is not dissimilar to my earlier historiographical study, this article is organised differently and aims to offer a synthesis of research approaches and research challenges. There is a greater focus on the research methodologies, and on the theoretical perspectives, utilised by historians of education. The article is organised in two sections: 'God's empire: the mission imperative in the history of education' and 'Monastic and conventual education: a growth area in historical scholarship'. Both sections provide a discussion of literature in the field, and some commentary on approaches and methodologies used by historians of education.

Religion has been, and continues to be, a major theme in the history of education, which scholars approach through research on many more areas than those discussed in this article. The limits of space, and the need to draw on areas in which I can claim some small expertise, mean that this article does not discuss myriad other areas that historians of education work on, such as religious movements, and denominational schooling. However, this journal will provide an excellent platform for new research perspectives on these and other important areas.

2   God's Empire: the Mission Imperative in the History of Education

The involvement of Christian missionaries in education has attracted the attention of scholars in the West for some fifty years, even at a time when mission history *per se* was suffering a loss of interest amongst scholars. The demise in scholarship on missions reflected a move towards 'rejecting explanatory factors drawn from the European arena' in favour of concentration on localities, local conditions, and 'internal studies', that drew attention away from 'the interplay of missions and empire' (Porter 2004, 4). By the 1980s, what Porter calls the 'overwhelmingly secular preoccupations of the academy' (ibid., 5) allowed little space for nuanced considerations of the relationship between empire and the Western mission imperative. Indeed, these 'secular preoccupations' also contributed to the neglect of what Harold Silver called 'the religious experience' in the history of education (Silver 1992, 97).

However, historians of education have demonstrated a sustained interest in mission history, and a robust literature has developed since the 1990s. Scholars have shown interest in understanding the place of mission history within religious and ecclesiastical history; others have examined mission organisations (Stanley 1992; Bartle 1994; Walsh 1995; Hewitt 1997; O'Connor *et al* 2000; Ward and Stanley eds 2000; Murphy 2000). In some cases, these historical accounts have been undertaken to mark an anniversary of a mission society or foundation (Stanley 1992; Ward and Stanley eds 2000). Influential missionary figures, including the explorer David Livingstone, the Catholic Bishop Shanahan in Nigeria, and the Anglican educator and minister Rev James Long in India, have demanded attention (Jordan 1949; Langmore 1989; Anderson *et al* 1994; Smyth 1994; O'Connor 1990; Oddie 1999; Ross 2002). Anniversary publications and biographical studies tend to follow a chronological narrative, but buried within such linear accounts are insights into ways in which preachers, priests and pupils experienced mission schooling at different times.

The vast literature on Christian missionaries shows very clearly that education was central to the activity of Catholic and Protestant missionaries. The Franciscan Order of Friars established a mission on the Florida coast in 1528, under the direction of a Spaniard, Father Juan Suarez. The Jesuits, who made their first mission to North America in 1606, expanded to found centres of education along the Mississippi, and in Illinois, during the seventeenth century. Following their suppression and restoration, they expanded in Louisiana and in the nineteenth century they founded schools in Montana and Idaho. With their long tradition of teaching, the principles of which were set out in 1599 in their *Ratio Studiorum*, they influenced the teaching methods and training programmes used by other European missionaries.

As Walls has noted, the 'first generation of the Protestant missionary enterprise was ... an evangelical undertaking', with a strong tradition of preaching (Walls 2009, 80). However, the potential for evangelisation and conversion through schooling was not lost on Protestant missionaries, and by the 1830s

Christian missionary schools were expanding rapidly (Smyth 1994; Inglesby 2000; Murphy 2000). Research shows that 'the members and agents of the missionary societies which began to form by the end of the century, were desperately concerned with action' (Walls 2009, 61). Walls has suggested that, unlike the Catholic Jesuit missionaries for example, the first generation of Protestant missionaries 'did not possess a high degree of formal education' (Walls 2009, 188). For example, only once in its first sixty years did the CMS send a university graduate to Africa. However, by the middle of the nineteenth century, Protestant missionary men were increasingly likely to have attended a public school or university, and some began to publish 'researches' that recounted their travels and observations, thereby contributing to a more scholarly image. These works included Livingstone's *Missionary Travels and Researches in South Africa* (1857), and *Polynesian Researches* (1829) by William Ellis. The rapid expansion of the nineteenth-century missionary movement has been discussed by Hogan (1990), Dries (1998), Murphy (2000), Porter (2004), and Humphries (2010). Though much scholarship focuses on missions and education in India and Africa, some historians of education have examined religious involvement in schooling in colonial America (Murphy 2000; Butler 2012; McGuinness 2013), and in Australia and New Zealand (Manion 1975; O'Donoghue 2001; Cumming 1985; Fitzgerald 2003; 2005; Morrison 2011).

The relationship between mission and the imperial past has received considerable treatment. Overwhelmingly the perspective taken by scholars writing on missionary activity has been to position their findings within discourse on colonialism (Raftery 2012). Historians have examined the work of mission schools as an arm of imperialism, exploring themes such as cultural imperialism, social control and the creation of 'colonial subjects' (Whitehead 1995; Takeshi and Mangan 1997; Bara 2005; Evans 2008; Hall 2008; Watts 2009; Allender 2010; 2017). Whitehead has made a significant contribution to research in this area, including examining Christian missionary efforts in British colonial education (1999). Of particular value to researchers is Whitehead's historiographical work, which discusses research on the involvement by missions in India and in Africa, and the working relations between missions and the British Government. Whitehead made a plea for a 'dispassionate and objective assessment of colonial education' (Whitehead 1995, 447). As I have noted elsewhere, this perspective could usefully be brought to bear in researching the involvement of missionaries and their legacy to education. Generally, scholars have found it easy to adopt a critical position towards the involvement of the various Churches in education, with the result that it has become unpopular (or not 'politically correct', to borrow from Whitehead) to find anything noteworthy in Church interference in learning (Raftery 2012).

Interdisciplinary work, utilising the methodologies and approaches of both anthropologists and historians, has shone light on the delivery and reception of missionary education (Bowie, Kirkwood and Ardener 1993; Labode 1993). Far from only evaluating missionaries in their field of operation, some historians have examined the influence of missions on British social history, and on the relationship of Britons to the concept of race. Indeed, Catherine Hall (2002) has argued that missions played a role in popularising empire amongst the British public. Importantly, scholars are also examining motives for missionary activity that do not reduce such activity to some part of the imperial project or its consequences. Women's history has made a contribution in this regard, by bringing the motives, agency and work of women missionaries into the frame (Leach 2008; Allender 2017). The involvement of Anglican women, some of whom were simply known as missionary 'wives', has attracted attention, as has a range of female mission societies (Fitzgerald 2003, 2005; Leach 2008). The work of Tim Allender, utilising Indian archives and adopting a feminist critique of education and empire, examines women's life experiences, to comment on ways in which colonial mentalities shaped their experiences of learning and teaching. His work uncovers ways in which women teachers in colonial India, including Roman Catholic teaching Sisters, pushed against boundaries of race, class, caste and religion. By looking 'outside the mission compound', Allender uncovers evidence of ways in which women missionaries 'crossed state-established racial divides and renegotiated education for girls' (Allender 2016, 146).

Rather than conducting comparative work, historians of education have tended to research specific geographical areas, or individual mission agencies and institutions. For example, Pearce (1988), Garvey (1994), Mwiria (1991), Kallaway (2009), Carmody (1999; 2000; 2016), Leach (2008) and Allen (2008) have examined African contexts. Other historians have examined mission activity in South Asia, Southeast Asia, Oceania, North America, and the Caribbean (Chiu 2998; Rooke 1980; 1994; Bartle 1994; Walsh 1995; Coleman 1996, Prochner et al 2009; Lee 2016), and the impact of Western education and missionaries in the Middle East (Tejirian and Simon 2002; Ment 2011). There is, however, room for much more comparative work, such as that of Michael Coleman (1996), who has done substantial work on Anglican mission schools for Native American children. In an innovative article, he compared his American data with material from Irish archives, and found similarities in ways in which proselytising Anglican missionaries removed Irish and 'American Indian' children from their homes, in order to raise them in orphan schools.

Generally, historians of education have paid more attention to Protestant missionary educators and education, and indeed with Protestant organisations that were involved in Christian education movements (Arthur 2019). Further, there is evidence that some scholars use the term 'Christian' when writing about what is in fact 'Protestant' missionary history, in a way that excludes the long tradition of Roman Catholic involvement in global missionary projects. Walls (2009), for example, might better have replaced 'Christian' with 'Protestant and Dissenting' in the title of his award-winning study, *The Missionary Movement in Christian History*, as modern Catholic mission history is absent. Titles of mission histories are equally misleading in terms of how inclusive they are in surveying both men's and women's involvement in missionary work. Hall's work is largely about men. Murphy's magisterial volume, *A History of Irish Emigrant and Missionary Education* (2000) pays scant attention to women missionaries and Sisters, while the title of Hogan's *The Irish Missionary Movement* (1990), which examines the contributions of Protestant and Catholic men, is misleading. Indeed, there is room for research on Catholic mission experience, and especially research on women religious (Sisters) whose work in the global Christian mission field has been ignored by historians of education. Additionally, there is room for more work on the reception of missionary education, and responses to missionary teachers, such as can be seen in the work of Lee (2013; 2016), which analyses Australian Presbyterian missionary activity in Korea. The use of oral accounts and the interrogation of the visual record of missionary education are two other areas that merit attention in scholarship.

3   **Monastic and Conventual Education: New Approaches in Historical Scholarship**

In 2010, a historiography of teaching Sisters was completed by Bart Hellinckx *et al*, as part of the *Studia Paedagogica* series. Entitled *The Forgotten Contribution of the Teaching Sisters: A Historiographical Essay on the Educational Work of Catholic Women Religious in the 19th and 20th Centuries*, it was a work that commenced by concurring with the view of historian Catriona Clear that 'Nuns have suffered the fate of historical marginalisation' (Clear 1987, xvii). The situation has certainly improved since the 1990s when Smyth predicted that 'the research on the history of teaching Sisters is just beginning' (Smyth 1994, 112). One of the main tasks of scholars working in this area, was to provide balance to a historical narrative that had overwhelmingly focussed on male monastic life, the contribution of individual bishops and priests to schools and colleges, and the role of the (male) Church hierarchy in education generally.

Until the 1980s, most research on teaching Sisters tended to provide readers with either hagiographical accounts of 'important' nuns, or chronological histories of convent schools. Some of these publications were written by male clergy or past pupils, and some were jubilee volumes (Hutch 1875; Gibbons 1928; Dowd and Tearle 1973; Forest 2004; Fox 2006; Galvin 1968; Yap 2001). Often, when Sisters were allowed to write biographical studies of Sisters, their books were published anonymously (Anon 1924: Anon 1961). More recently, as noted by Raftery (2013), there has been a move towards work that seeks to position the history of women religious within the history of education and women's history (Curtis 2000; Rogers 2005; Mangion 2005). Teaching congregations have invited lay historians to write their histories (Ryllis Clark 2009; Garaty 2013; Raftery, Delaney and Nowlan-Roebuck 2019). Such work has dispelled the worn-out stereotype of the Catholic nun as the 'obedient, meek, humble servant of the male-dominated church' (Ebaugh 1993, 402).

Globally, there are scholars working on many teaching orders of Sisters. Smyth (2007) and Bruno-Jofré (2005) have worked on teaching orders in Canada; Curtis (2000), Kilroy (2000; 2012) and Rogers (1998; 2005) have written on French women religious in education; and Coburn and Smith (1999) and McGuinness (2013) on nuns in the United States, have all greatly illuminated our understanding of what women religious contributed to teaching, the building of schools, and educational leadership more generally. In Britain and Ireland, scholarship on women religious and education has been a growth area in research particularly since the 1990s, and includes the work of Raughter (1995), Peckham Magray (1998), Kealy (2007), Luddy (2012) and Raftery (2012; 2013; 2015). A common tension in the life of teaching Sisters is finding a balance between being a 'good teacher' and a 'good religious', and this has been explored by Mangion (2005) in her study of British convents. In the Irish context, studies of Catholic education have noted that some religious congregations affiliated their schools to the national system in order to benefit from State grants and aid. For example, scholars have examined how the Presentation Sisters, who founded dozens of schools in Ireland, affiliated their schools to the national system without compromising the Catholic ethos of their schools (Raftery and Nowlan-Roebuck 2007; Raftery, Delaney and Nowlan-Roebuck 2019; Raftery 2019).

There have been new turns in scholarship on women religious, that include both theoretical and methodological innovations. The global reach of teaching Sisters interests a number of scholars, some of whom have used the lens of transnationalism in their work (Burley 2012; Raftery 2013, 2015; Collins 2015). Margaret MacCurtain's plea that historians should 'hear the voices of women religious' (MacCurtain 1995, 58) has been noted, and oral histories of teaching Sisters add a richness to our understanding of female education conducted by Sisters. (Casey 1993; McKenna 2006). Innovative methodologies are evident in the work of Collins (2015), who used a 'collective biography' approach in her study of a group of Dominican Sisters involved in education in New Zealand from the 1930s to the 1960s. Additionally, interpretive challenges have been met, such as finding ways of using account books to assess the economic 'value' of the labour of Sisters (Van Dijck *et al*, 2012), and obituaries to construct analyses of their lives (Burley 2012). Scholarship has also tackled the questions around identity (Rogers 1998; Mangion 2005). Symbolism, culture and convent school ideologies have been the focus of work by Trimingham Jack (1998) and Lei (2000).

Historians have also worked on challenging areas, where records are often slender, such as the study of lay Sisters (Trimingham Jack 2000), and research on early monastic life for women (Bowden 1999; 2005; Gervais and Watson 2014). Bowden, in 'Community space and cultural transmission: formation and schooling in English enclosed convents in the seventeenth century' (2005), drew on a range of little-known archival sources for 22 convents occupied by English nuns in exile. She also scrutinised the use of space within convents, examining plans and architectural drawings, for her analysis of how 'separation' and 'enclosure' were part of the gendered management of women in convents. Gervais and Watson (2014), have worked on monastic life for women in the twentieth century, using Michel Foucault's conception of monastic discipline in their analysis of oral histories of women religious. They have added nuance and balance by drawing on Ann Cvetkovich's understanding of the 'utopia of everyday habit', in their argument that women experienced convent life as complicated and restrictive, but also as generative, and imbued with affective possibilities (Gervais and Watson 2014, 7–10). By studying the oral accounts of a large sample of teaching sisters, Gervais and Watson concluded that the routines and regulations of convent life were differentially experienced. Their work demands that other scholars working in this area become attuned to the myriad ways in which teaching sisters 'lived' their vocation to religious life alongside their teaching vocation. Indeed, they are critical of the absence of women religious from the 'androcentric historical and contemporary accounts of the Catholic Church' (ibid), noting that where women religious are included, their work is often trivialized.

The trivialisation of the work of teaching Sisters is one of the reasons that they have been almost completely erased from social history, Church history, and the history of education, a situation which is only now—slowly—being ameliorated. There remains, however, an obstacle to a full and nuanced understanding of the global work of teaching Sisters: sometimes researchers find it impossible to gain access to relevant archives. The archives of religious communities are private collections, therefore researchers are very much guests of the community. Access can only be granted when there is a Sister able to take time away from her many other responsibilities to facilitate a researcher. Until comparatively recently, few congregations had the resources to hire professional archivists, and their records were simply not ready for scholars. The problem of limited access for historians of education to religious archives has been discussed by Smyth (1994), Trimingham Jack (2000), O'Donoghue and Potts (2004), Raftery and Nowlan-Roebuck (2007), O'Donoghue and Chapman (2011), and Raftery (2011). There is evidence that the situation is improving, particularly where congregations have centralised their collections, appointed lay archivists, and—in some cases—begun to digitise parts of their collections (Raftery 2017). It is in these archives that much can be learned about ways in which religious history and the history of education are intertwined.

4   Conclusion

Historians of education have shown a sustained interest in missionary education, in its various forms. There is also a strong body of literature that examines, and critiques, the involvement of various Christian missionary groups in education. Scholars have been attentive to both the impact of these missionary initiatives on the imperial project, and the ways in which mission societies and congregations operated in their countries of origin. While scholarship in the key journals that disseminate research on the history of education has betrayed an Anglo-centric viewpoint, this is changing, and the focus in these journals on the history of Protestants and Dissenting groups is also changing. A notable growth area in research is scholarship on the history of Catholic teaching religious. The energies of scholarly societies, and the imbrication of women's history, the history of education, and the history of women religious, have benefited the dissemination of new scholarship on teaching Sisters and convent education.

Over the past fifty years, historians of education have moved from narrative accounts of schooling, to nuanced studies that draw on methodological innovations, and different theoretical perspectives. When the historian of education, Harold Silver, drew attention to the need to bring 'the Catholic, the Christian, the religious experience into the canon of educational history' (Silver 1992), he made a clarion call for the kind of work that will animate debate going forward, and encourage researchers to contribute to journals such as this journal on research perspectives in R&E.

Religion and Education: Mapping the Field (a Philosophical Approach)

David Lewin

1   Introduction

In this section I will examine the relations of R&E from a distinctly philosophical perspective. My aim is to provide key elements of a philosophical consideration of these relations, whilst offering some perspective on historical and contemporary debates that form the 'state of the art.' A full account of this would require an exploration of the relations between R&E in diverse philosophical and conceptual terms across the globe, however this is not feasible within the limited scope of this section. I cannot avoid forms of generalisation and reduction, and the somewhat arbitrary and rather parochial understandings that frame them. So, completeness is not my aim. I will not, for instance, discuss the philosophical principles of Catholic Education in Hong Kong (e.g. Chan 2015), Muslim Education in Turkey (e.g. Ozgur 2012), or the recent emergence of religious education in Russia (Blinkova and Vermeer 2018). Nor will I explore broader questions of neutrality in religious education in Canada (e.g. Cormier 2018) or issues concerning social justice in religious education in South Africa (e.g. van der Walt 2011). Both the terms *religion* and *education* mean different things in these different contexts and their relation has different resonances wherever one goes.

To limit my scope, I have chosen to address philosophical and conceptual questions that throw light on the constructed character of religion and education as categories. It must be acknowledged that the form of the questions and, more particularly, my frames of reference, are formed within my own context as a researcher within the UK and the philosophies of education developed therein. While I acknowledge this situatedness, I will structure my discussion around what I take to be two basic questions pertinent to this study: namely 'what is religion?' and 'what is education?' Before addressing these two questions, I will consider what distinguishes my approach from the others in this issue: What does it mean to look at R&E from a philosophical perspective? How can a philosophical approach help us to think about these concepts and their relation?

2 What Does It Mean to Ask about the Relations of Religion and Education in a Philosophical Way?

While there is no single agreed philosophical methodology, one central philosophical task is broadly ontological: raising the question of what a thing is.[1] Acknowledging that the reader has some general notion of the two 'objects' of our inquiry, R&E, as well as their relation, it is vitally important to consider the nature of these objects. Thus, we are engaged in a philosophical inquiry that acknowledges the interpretive approach to the objects of inquiry: we always already have some preliminary understandings that orient our inquiries, allowing us to look more closely at the objects themselves (Gadamer, Weinsheimer, & Marshall, 2004). The regular refrain lamenting the lack of religious literacy in contemporary society draws attention to the possibility that our preliminary views of religion may be rather simplistic and parochial ("Religious Literacy Project," ND). Some views of the matter are prone to blame religion for many social ills while other kinds of oversimplification hope that religion can provide a direct answer to those ills. The more academically inclined draw attention to the ways that 'religion' has been constructed in the image of the prevailing analytical frame in relation to the emergence of Religious Studies as an academic field (Cotter and Robinson 2016; Owen 2016). These preliminary interpretations don't just provide answers, but also questions that frame the debate (Aldridge, 2015, pp. 5–13). It pays to consider first how the subject is framed by looking at how the relations between religion and education are treated in general terms.

In the discipline of Religious Studies taxonomies are never far away and provide a useful entry point (Cotter and Robinson 2016). Anna Strhan provides a helpful taxonomy of literature in the field of R&E, offering five general headings: religious upbringing; religious education and the curriculum; faith-based schools; issues of religious identity; religious philosophies of education (Strhan, ND). Strhan points out that many debates concern the competing interests and rights of religious groups, parents, children, and the state, while showing that these discussions do not belong only to schooling, or parenting, but cut across all kinds of social interaction and formation. Questions of ethical justification have also been central in attempting to distinguish legitimate forms of influence and formation from those that are not legitimate and which may alternatively be called manipulation or indoctrination (see, for instance, Hand, 2018; Tillson, 2019).

---

1 It should be remembered that, strictly speaking, 'ontology' concerns the nature of being as such rather than how some particular thing is understood, which is a more general question.

Like religion the term *education* is laden with everyday meanings that both help and hinder attempts to understand the relations of R&E in philosophical terms. The association of education with schooling or with formal education, or the conflation of education with socialisation contribute to a rather confused picture of how education should be related to religion. I will focus this inquiry somewhat by reference to *forms of influence* across the life-course which, as John Tillson summarises, can be "systematic, ad hoc, aims-based, aimless, outcomes-focused, process-focused, incidental, intentional, unintentional, and much else besides" (Tillson, 2018, p. 1059). The neutrality implied in the concept of influence encourages us to recognise that it can be "anti-religious, pro-religious, or neutral about the value of religion" (Tillson, 2018, p. 1059). This is significant for two reasons.

First, I wish to present an account of educational influence that is not normatively charged: I want to avoid the idea that 'education' refers to forms of influence that I happen to agree with (or believe to be good), while reserving other terms, e.g. indoctrination or propaganda, for those forms of influence I happen not agree with. Admittedly, I will discuss forms of influence (e.g. advertising) that do not qualify as being *education* by referring to the idea that they serve the interests of the influencer, with no particular concern for the 'influencee'. But this describes relations of intention concerning *who* is being influenced, not whether the influence itself can be defined as good (or otherwise). To have a descriptive idea of education as influence helps us to see that even objectionable forms of influence employ educational concepts, structures and relations (e.g. Nazi education is not a contradiction in terms because the Nazi educator intends something good for the influencee).

Second, when thinking about definitions of religion there is a tendency to see religious influence as substantially different from other forms of influence (moral, political, aesthetic, and so on), or, at least deserving of special critical attention. In contrast to this, I will argue that it is helpful to see religious influence as continuous with other forms, a point that is related to the other critical idea here: that we ought not to define religion in too narrow terms (for instance, defined as assent to certain propositions about the world).

This brief outline highlights a central argument of this section: that how R&E are constructed has consequences on how we understand their interaction. Therefore, rather than moving directly into an examination of the justifications for religious upbringing, or against faith schools, or for different forms of religious education in the curriculum, a philosophical approach compels us to examine more carefully the constructions that shape these debates in the first place (Lewin, 2017a). Whether we see R&E as natural friends or enemies, or whether we resist such binaries, depends to a significant degree, on the conditions and assumptions in which the debates take place. While answers to questions like 'what are legitimate forms of influence?' are numerous and relatively unstable, the formulation of the question is a more constant feature of educational theory. Despite the relative longevity of the questions of R&E, the conditions in which the questions are asked shift as society comes to terms with historical changes: for instance, with the movements like the 'death of God' in the nineteenth century and the much more recent 'return of religion.' Thus, I seek to draw attention to some of the changing conditions in which questions are raised.

As well as examining what the objects of inquiry are, philosophy also raises teleological questions. Consideration of the purpose, end or meaning of something is important in establishing the evaluative or normative conditions which guide the inquiry, and where normative concerns reappear. Nazi education might be good for certain outcomes (outcomes that we would agree are bad). In the sphere of human action and what might be called the *human sciences* (as distinct from natural sciences[2]) we need to consider what we take to be of value, or 'good', in order to consider the purpose, end, or meaning of a thing. The necessity of this consideration is quite obvious in the context of educational influence: we can only evaluate a particular educational event when we have (or are prepared to commit to) some conception of what good influences looks like; when, in other words, we have some conception of the purposes or ends of education (Biesta, 2010). The justification for educational influence requires reference to the substantive good that comes from that kind of influence (Gutmann, 1982).

To summarise, as educators we are engaged in formative influences and it is a philosophical task to reflect on the nature, purpose, and justification of these forms of influence. The context of the interaction between R&E provides, if not unique, certainly very significant contexts for examining these kinds of influence and the justifications we have for them.

3   General Conceptual Issues

I have acknowledged the presence of guiding ideas about religion, education and their relation, ideas which give shape and form to our questions and interpretations, but can also inhibit reflection on the proper relations that may exist between education and religion. These ideas have underpinned philosophical

---

2 The concept of human sciences invoked here places the considerations within the broad tradition of philosophical hermeneutics. See (Ricoeur & Thompson, 1981).

debates about the place of religion in education throughout the history of philosophy in the work of figures from Plato to Augustine to Rousseau and so on. More recent discussions of these concerns have addressed the rights and wrongs of different forms of religious influence from Paul Hirst and others (Hirst, 1974; Marples, 1978). As mentioned already, these debates have often focused on the competing rights between children, parents, religious groups, and the state (Brighouse, 2006; Strhan, ND), and to what extent and under what conditions forms of (religious) influence can be justified (Tillson, 2019). Some have argued, for instance, that faith schools are necessarily indoctrinatory (Hand, 2003; Siegel, 2004), others, that faith schools can, and often do, pay sufficient attention to the development of critical faculties to avoid this charge (Thiessen, 1993), and still others, that indoctrination is a term that applies not to religious forms of influence specifically, but applies to the process of instilling any kind of ideas or values "into the unwilling or unaware" (Copley, 2008, p. 25). Whether the issue of indoctrination hinges upon the extent to which a religious perspective is 'exclusivist' (asserting the claims of one particular religious tradition to the necessary exclusion of all other possible claims) is a matter of discussion and interpretation (Wareham, 2017), though it seems fair to say that exclusivist religious views are more likely to inculcate forms of closed-mindedness that inhibit criticality and autonomy (Callan & Arena, 2010). Questions of indoctrination cut across a range of relevant issues here, from religious upbringing, to religious education in the curriculum, to faith schools, and therefore represent a fundamental concern. But questions of indoctrination both arise out of, and reinforce, a certain construction of R&E.

Debates about the ethics of indoctrination emerge within a construction of religion characterised as the "world religions paradigm" (Owen 2016), in which world religions offer competing truth claims or differing accounts of *how things are*. These accounts of seem to place religions in competition with each other and with other accounts of *how things are*, such as scientific accounts: science is then seen to be in conflict with religion, and, typically, religious ideas lose out to scientific advances. There is a body of work undertaken in the field of religion and science that complicates this 'conflict' view of the relation, by suggesting that accounts of *how things are* are not commensurable, working in different ways and representing different, reconcilable perspectives (Barbour, 1998; Haught, 1995; Polkinghorne, 1995). Religious accounts of *how things are* may be said to exist at a different level of analysis, or, to use Wittgensteinian terms, are formed within different language games.

The last 50 years have also seen considerable changes to our understanding of the place of religion in culture and education which gives context to our present discussion, from the rise of Religious Studies alongside traditional

Theology among the academic disciplines (Smart, 1998), to the shift from confessional religious education (hereafter RE) to non-confessional RE, to increased global tensions in the wake of an emergent narrative of a clash of civilisations to the most recent recognition of the 'return of religion' that has sometimes been called the post-secular (Gearon, 2013; Lewin, 2017a, 2017c). The field of the sociological analysis of religion has become increasingly influential and difficult to disentangle from the theological and philosophical discussions amidst a more politicised social landscape, and has led to speculation about whether recent discussions about the place of religion in education are really talking about the same thing when using the terms *religion* and *belief* (Lewin, 2017b, 2017c). In order to address some of these issues we now move more directly to the objects of inquiry themselves, starting with conceptual questions: What is religion? What is education? How are these two things properly related? These inquiries form the foundational ideas that shape discussions of a range of questions from religious upbringing to religious education and the curriculum, from faith-based schools to the wider influence of religion on education structures and practices.

4   What Is Religion?

How are we to distinguish religious phenomena from other kinds of phenomena? Is mindfulness a religious practice? Does Jediism count as a religion? Is Bhagwan Shree Rajneesh a religious figure? How does the rise of different forms of non-religion fit in to an account of religion? There are no easy answers to questions like these. Nevertheless, when educators represent phenomena to their students, selections and simplifications must be made, and some kind of framework seems necessary (Lewin 2019). The emergence of the so-called "world religions paradigm" (Owen 2016) offers a framework which "conceptualises religious ideas and practice as being configured by a series of major religious systems, that can be clearly identified as having discrete characteristics" (Suthren Hirst and Zavos 2005, 5). In other words, religions are constructed. We think in terms of (normally 5 or so) major world religions which share, broadly speaking, similar defining features (deities, texts, founding figures etc.).

But that which is constructed can also be deconstructed, and if we deconstruct them, we are more able to examine what goes into them, and reflect on the work they do, the interests they serve, and the effects they have. Indeed, many scholars of religion have examined the ways in which our organisation of world religions is a product of a particular Western orientalist construction (Said 1978) which emerged in the nineteenth century in order to distinguish

Western religions from others (Cox, 2007; Masuzawa, 2005; Owen 2016).
A charitable hermeneutic would interpret these constructions as arising out
of a pedagogical concern, though we would be naïve to deny that these representations also reflect socio-political attitudes and hegemonies. Examining
these constructions brings us to a focus on curricular representation (which is
only one of a number of ways of thinking about the relations between R&E).
But it also raises general philosophical issues concerning the way understanding entails essentialization and decontextualization (Geaves 2005), and how
"the aura of comparable qualities" can be, as Bell argues, "historically and
theologically misleading" (Bell 2006, 34). What follows, then, are some comments that consider how our constructions of religion shape the interaction
between R&E.

The Oxford dictionary defines religion as "belief in and worship of a super-
human controlling power, especially a personal God or gods" (Dictionaries).
This initial construction, focusing on belief and worship of something super-
human, may not include everything that we might want to interpret in religious terms (Billington, 2002), but provides a reasonable point of departure.
Hand has defined religion as belief in a god or gods that have some positive relevance (Hand, 2006, pp. 93–99). This seems broadly consistent with the initial
dictionary definition, but such definitions raise further questions: what does
it mean to believe something? The dictionary defines *belief* as "an acceptance
that something exists or is true, especially one without proof" (Dictionaries).
This appeal to truth is rooted in the idea that what makes a *proposition* 'true'
is its correspondence with what is the case. The truth lies within a propositional claim or statement which must be verified against what is actual. While
this kind of correspondence model of truth has objections (David, 2016) it locates truth in propositions that require a certain kind of cognitive assent, a
"propositional view" of religion that ought not to be taken as the only way of
understanding religion (Lewin, 2017a). Certainly, there is much in religious life
that appears to be determined by cognitive assent to certain propositions: for
example, the beliefs in God's existence, Jesus' resurrection, etc. However, there
is more to the lived experience of religious people than this kind of assent. But
the construction of religion as propositional has distinct consequences for the
nature of the discussion of R&E.

Firstly, it encourages the idea that religions seek to use education to disseminate or reinforce doctrinal positions. Seeking to influence in this way has
sometimes been associated with undermining autonomy where that influence
is regarded as a restriction of critical inquiry (i.e. the idea of an obedience to
faith). But what if we understand religion differently? What if religious life is
conceived in terms of belonging rather than believing, as some scholars have

put it (McIntosh 2015)? We still notice that there are influences to encourage people to belong, but the nature of that influence could be understood differently than the kind of influence to accept as true certain statements about the world.

Secondly, this cognitive and propositional view of religion tends to frame religion in 'absolutist' and 'exclusivist' terms which results in a view succinctly expressed by Philip Barnes, that "if the beliefs of one religion are true, the beliefs of some other religion (or religions) must be false" (Barnes, 2008, p. 70). An exclusivist view of religion seems to correlate with common-sense (Wainwright, 2005): Christians believe that Christ is the one and only incarnation of God; Muslims believe that the Qu'ran is God's final revelation; Jews begin morning prayers thanking God for not having been made heathen and so on. Exclusivism extends to forms of polytheism and atheism: the eternal Dharma of Vedic Hinduism pronounces that the almighty power of the Supreme Divinities is only Brahman; Buddhists take only the eightfold path to Enlightenment, and even atheists are committed to the non-existence of God.

This exclusivism might seem consistent with state-sponsored RE where faith formation could plausibly be exclusively confessional (widespread across Europe before the 1960's), and is associated with national identity. Here RE is more likely to be regarded as a kind of protection of the forming religious subject (e.g. the Catholic child is protected against the heresies of the Protestant sects). While historical contexts do not justify the principle of exclusivism, it helps us understand its existence and legacy. However, with the shift to non-confessional, multi-faith RE pioneered since the 1960's a very different social context has emerged in which contact with other groups, traditions and religious cultures demands something else of RE (Cush, 2018).

What does pluralism demand of RE? This difficult question remains unresolved. On the face of it, pluralism might simply encourage tolerance of, and engagement with, difference. However, for some 'critical theorists,' the terms of engagement with the 'other' fundamentally undermine the condition of authentic religious identity: that ultimate truth is at stake (Barnes, 2008; Barnes & Wright, 2006; Barnes, 2011). The binary conditions which Barnes and Wright demand for the subject of RE has been called a "return to the old discourse" (Owen 2016, 264) concerning the (Christian) truth, a kind of nostalgia for 'proper' faith formation. Owen associates these conditions with a doctrinal construction of religion, in which religious identity hinges on competing and irreconcilable doctrines (Owen 2016). No wonder that for these critical theorists, pluralist RE is a contradiction.

There are other ways of understanding religious pluralism, from functionalist views that pluralism fosters social cohesion, to philosophical views that a stark opposition between 'outsiders' and 'insiders' misunderstands the nature of religious identity and language (Davis, 2010), to theological understandings of the nature of religious knowledge and experience as akin to aesthetic knowing rather than propositional truth claims (Lewin, 2017a). Religious pluralism is an inevitable outcome of the recognition that religions are constructed. The link between the doctrinal/propositional and exclusivist/absolutist conceptions of religion is summarised by Morimoto:

> If religion is all about giving assent to these divisive sets of doctrines, there is little chance for us to understand each other well. But if religion is primarily a matter of trust, piety, devotion, loyalty and commitment, then we all are somehow able to perceive what we have in common, regardless of tradition. The content of faith may be different, but its quality is similar; and this awareness of similarity may hopefully cultivate within us a kind of empathy towards each other.
>
> MORIMOTO, 2005, p. 180

This is not the place to fully explore whether this focus on what is common erodes the nature of religion as such, but should at least signal that there are different ways of thinking about the nature of religion, ways that affect how we interpret the place of religion in education.

As well as having an impact upon curricula considerations around RE, the assertion of an absolute and exclusive religious identity also correlates with tensions around the existence of faith schools. The more exclusive our view of the matter, the more essential it becomes to find a way of mediating differences in the public square, or rather, the more important it is to maintain mutual respect through the establishment of impartial secular public. This is not the place to rehearse the (Christian) history of the construction of secularism and the modern "formations of the secular" (see Asad, 2003). Nevertheless, these constructions generally seek to enforce a demarcation of religious identity and public life: that the need for the protection of religious groups emerges as religions are viewed as competing with one another. Given that common or comprehensive schools are public institutions, one approach to the organisation of religious schools could be that they give no preference to any absolutist and exclusivist religious claims (McLaughlin, Carr, Halstead, & Pring, 2008). This might be interpreted to mean that faith schools are, in principle, unjustified. But this interpretation concedes the view of religion as exclusivist. Furthermore, this view fails to acknowledge the conditions in which the concept of the secular is formed: emerging out of a Western Christian intellectual history (Asad, 2003). The attempt to create a "zone of absence" (Warner,

VanAntwerpen, & Calhoun, 2010, p. 8) for the protection of legal, political, and educational independence, free of religious influence, reinforces a narrow account of what it means to be religious, and does not acknowledge the many forms of (pseudo-)religiosity evident within secular culture. As James Smith has argued, secular culture could be regarded as forming people through its own kind of secular liturgical practices (J. Smith, K. A., 2009). An ancillary issue that results from this debate is the tendency to reduce education to schooling, since 'private' forms of upbringing (e.g. parenting, informal education etc.) tend to be left out of the debates about public education, particularly the rather hackneyed discussions concerning the justifications for faith schools in the UK, discussions that are far from settled (Pring, 2018).

The exclusivist construction of religion can be deconstructed.[3] Exclusivism belongs particularly to a kind of propositional view of language and doctrinal view of religion in which statements of belief such as 'I believe in life after death,' exclude rival beliefs, e. g. 'I believe that my life ends when I die.' Hand understands religion to be about rival propositional beliefs: "[t]he differences between the followers of different religious and irreligious paths are fundamentally differences of belief: the followers assent to different propositions about what the world is like" (Hand, 2015, p. 36). For Hand, these differences of belief are typically called religious when they involve a theory of the world, or worldview, that entails "an account of the significance, origin and purpose of human existence" (Hand, 2012, p. 529). This 'worldview' understanding of religion embodies an exclusivist position, since Christian origins and purposes are generally inconsistent with, or rival to, other accounts. On this basis, Hand argues that "faith schools are objectionable because they attempt to secure children's assent to epistemically controversial propositions" (Hand, 2012, p. 536). Such a view raises the question of how one can distinguish controversial propositions from non-controversial propositions.

Is the ancient Egyptian view that 'The sky is a cow' controversial? Wilfred Cantwell-Smith argues that a true/false binary is not the best way of understanding what ancient Egyptians meant when they made this claim (W. C. Smith, 1998, p. 14). Controversy is not an absolute property, but one relative to the cultural norms that govern what counts as reasonable in a given context. When we consider the fact that there are no absolute criteria for determining what is controversial, we should be aware that there are no simple ways of distinguishing the kinds of teaching that should be directive (e.g. that the square

---

3 This 'view of religion' can also include forms of *non-religion* such as atheism. Some forms of atheism are certainly absolutist and exclusivist in nature which ought to reveal tendencies towards dogmatism do not belong only to religious ideas.

of the hypotenuse is equal to the sum of the squares of the other two sides) from those that should be non-directive (e.g. patriotism or national values). The presence or absence of rival views is not a sufficient condition for determining what is controversial, nor, I think, the suggestion that a significant majority hold a particular view. But the debates around the search for epistemic criterion (criteria that distinguish controversial from non-controversial issues) as it is sometimes called (Hand, 2008), may be missing a larger point since they tend to presuppose something that is, I suggest, questionable: that religious life is essentially about assent to propositions of a religious nature. Religious beliefs may be less about rival claims about the world, than varied social, ritual and devotional practices which express various meanings and commitments. While these are often, of course, related to beliefs, I remain convinced that there is more to belief than assent to truth claims. Just as different works us art disclose aspects of the world in different ways, so religious influences may offer new perspectives on a range of experiences. The idea that beliefs, including religious beliefs, ought to be a matter of rational persuasion (and that anything else is indoctrination) locates the nature of religion in the sphere of cognitive claim. This perspective often fails to see how far religious influence is bound up with other forms of influence: language, food and dress, the structure of work and play, indeed almost every sphere of social life is entangled with religious identity. And when we influence our children with respect to these other elements of social life, we are not so inclined to demand rational accounts as we do in the sphere of religion. Religious influence might, therefore, be less about securing assent to more or less controversial claims, than about learning to see, or live in a particular way. This is not to deny that there are better and worse (or more and less true) forms of seeing or living, nor that these influences also require justification, but to acknowledge that there is no absolute perspective from which all other views could be deemed false. Ninian Smart has been influential in shifting our perception of the nature of religion from a rather narrow Western construction of dogmatic and theological disputations. Smart was among the first to tell the history of this propositional reduction of religion: the religions of the book (Judaism, Christianity and Islam), being textually oriented since they share elements of the Hebrew Bible, have encouraged Western scholars to interpret other religions through the doctrinal/propositional lens (Smart, 1996). The legacy of this Western construction has been the tendency to interpret religions propositionally, thereby encouraging a binary true/false evaluation to be applied, and creating the conditions in which problems of exclusivism and absolutism become educationally problematic. Fern Elsdon-Baker (2015), for instance, has illustrated the ways in which framing questions in terms of binaries of belief, encourages us to overlook the nuances of religious commitment and tends to construct hardened faith positions in overly oppositional terms.

My general argument, then, is that the constructions of *religion* within education have led us to address certain problems and ask certain questions: questions of indoctrination and the competing claims of different groups (children, parents, communities and the state); questions of the nature of religious identity and RE in a pluralist context. In these debates there has been a tendency to overlook the constructed nature of religion in academic and educational discourse. These constructions require deconstruction, as does any elementary presentation of subject matter: as the student's understanding develops, the initial 'textbook' interpretation of the field must be critically examined and reinterpreted. But we appear, now, to focus on schooling. Why is it that discussions of education tend to lapse into the default context of the school? I now turn to the question of education to attempt to again broaden the scope of what is meant by education.

5   What Is Education?

Beyond schooling, I hope it is clear that the concept of *influence*[4] is central to the idea of education being discussed here. There are many kinds of influence, of course, some intentional, others accidental, some positive, others negative, some long-lasting, others transient. But not all influences are educational. For the purposes of my argument, the concept of *education* is defined as a particular form of influence that is necessarily *intentional*, one that intends a positive outcome for the person being influenced (the *influencee*). In other words: education is an intention to influence someone's relation to something in a positive way. Without the inclusion of the concept of *positive* influence (aka improvement or enhancement), we risk including forms of influence that could benefit the influencer while having negative effects on the influencee, for instance the advertiser who sells sugary drinks, knowing full well that the influence will not be good for the consumer, but that it will increase their own profit. Following Moles, this could be regarded as manipulation because it interferes with the preferences of the influencee by bypassing or undermining

---

4 The concept of influence might give an inaccurate picture of an active influencer and a passive 'influencee'. It is important to acknowledge that this does not describe a direct causal relation since human beings are not mechanical objects and respond in unpredictable ways to any influence. In other words, we may intend certain influences, but how those influences are 'taken up' is a complex matter beyond my present scope.

the way judgements and preferences are formed (Moles, 2015). In the case of the advertiser, the manipulation is exploitative (and therefore is not educational) if it ignores the good of the influencee. However, manipulation need not be exploitative in this way. Manipulation can be educational where it is in the interests of the influencee, for instance, where a teacher paternalistically manipulates certain conditions without necessarily sharing the full intentions of these actions with children. If these manipulations are educationally motivated, then they qualify as education. So, the question turns on whether the influences are educationally oriented: whether they intend to improve the student's conditions, capacities or relations with things/people. This helps us to determine which religious influences are, in principle, justifiable: whether they have the interests of the influencee in mind is a necessary (though not sufficient) condition for the justification of religious influence.

But how are we to make a judgement concerning what is in the interests of the influencee? Sincerity is not a reliable measure of veracity. Education is not a physical science, but a social, or better, *human* science, which means that there is a gap between intentions and outcomes. Education is a speculative or hermeneutic art (or science) since the outcomes of its influences always entail (uncertain) interpretive judgements. If the student experiences some change for the better then the precise causes of the change are difficult, perhaps impossible, to determine. This locates the significant educational questions again on intentions since they are able to be determined (or stated in learning outcomes, for instance). Intentions, or purposes, require some conception of the good life and so educators must exercise judgement in order to determine what they believe the good life looks like in order to know how to rightly organise their intentions to influence. Only rightly organised intentions to influence (governed by a commitment to the good) can be ethically justified since justification is derived from an orientation to the good. This makes ethical considerations central to educational theory and practice (Biesta, 2010).

These debates are also informed by political theory. Naturally, perhaps, liberal political theorists tend to regard the concept of influence with suspicion since it can appear to circumvent the process rational assessment. But where liberalism is valued, the formation of autonomy becomes a key concern. The common view of liberal theorists concerning upbringing is that, although children are initially not autonomous persons, upbringing ought to intend to bring about autonomy. Many argue that attitudes and beliefs of children can be shaped by parents and teachers as long as this kind of influence does not undermine the child's future capacity for autonomy (see Giesinger, 2013). The question of autonomy is of central significance for contemporary educational theory since it remains unclear what it is and why it ought to be the standard by forms of education are generally measured. Before examining what I will call 'autonomy vs religious influence' in greater detail (section 5 below), we must discuss further the nature and justification of specifically religious forms of influence.

In the sphere of education, the scope of concept of influence is broad. Addressing a narrower focus, Tillson asks what he calls a basic question: "how ought children to be influenced with respect to religion?" (Tillson, 2018, p. 1059). This question is restrictive in two respects: it focuses on *religious* influence and the influence of *children*. From my point of view, educational influence can be found wherever one person seeks to influence another, but the debate tends to be addressed to the influence of adults on children since this is the typical context of education. I have also sought to show that the question of the ethics of influence is not peculiar to religious influence. It is not clear why religion should be perceived as a special case of influence. It is important to see the question of influence cutting across politics, aesthetics and religion, but also to other social practices from language to diet. This is partly, but not only because in many contexts religious identity is more directly associated with diet or language, politics or aesthetics, than others.

I can intend to influence someone else by making a testimony of the effects that a given practice or belief has on my life, or through other means such as didactic instruction, role modelling, or encouraging and arranging encounters with people who behave or believe differently. My testimony could concern my vegan diet that I believe is giving me greater energy and lust for life. We don't normally consider this a *religious belief*, though, if we take the complications of what it means to be religious seriously, then it is not altogether clear how one justifies this distinction. One might argue that what makes belief 'religious' is that it concerns a general theory of the world, or worldview (Hand, 2012), and that it is therefore 'comprehensive' in scope, a concept that educational theorists sometimes draw from John Rawls (Rawls, 1996).[5] For instance, Matthew Clayton has argued that the idea of a "comprehensive enrolment"—of raising one's children in accordance with one's own conception of the good—is often illegitimate particularly where this kind of influence inhibits the autonomy of the child (Clayton, 2006).

---

5   Clayton (2012) argues that Rawls understands 'comprehensive' matters quite broadly, to include, religion, occupation, lifestyle, sexuality, though the concept of the 'comprehensive doctrine' seems to me to suggest grand theoretical views of things (Voice 2014).

Questions of the nature and extent of influence are core to philosophical issues of the ethics of influence. I can seek to influence another in rather restricted ways concerning rather uncontroversial things: I can encourage my son to try brussels sprouts. Eating brussels sprouts is not, as far as I know, controversial and will not, I suppose, entail a comprehensive change: it is unlikely to transform his worldview. But my influence is *educational*: my actions are guided by an intention to improve my son's relation to some object (sprouts) and activity (eating them). There are more or less effective ways of doing this, of course, but questions of effectiveness are not primarily philosophical, being more a matter of pedagogical knowledge and practice. Whether my intention to influence is successful or not, the actions (which might include manipulations) that encourage eating brussels sprouts in someone else (demonstrating exaggerated pleasure when eating sprouts) are of an educational nature. But the existence of certain forms of influence that are neither especially controversial nor comprehensive, like eating sprouts, should not lead us to assume that we can easily determine what is and what is not controversial and comprehensive.

What of saying grace before the meal that includes the aforementioned brassica? Is there an intention to improve another's relation to the world that is either controversial or comprehensive? In some situations, this would certainly seem inappropriate, awkward or unwelcome precisely because it holds more significance, and is relatively comprehensive in nature. A meal with children entails a good deal of influence, from the language spoken, to the food eaten, to the inculcation of table manners, to the festive atmosphere that may occasion the meal. What I take to be forms of religious influence shade off into other forms of influence with no clear boundaries separating them, especially where the definition of religion is not restricted to self-conscious assent to a set of cognitive truth claims or propositions. Consider also the (pseudo-)spiritual practices that have become very popular in recent years: meditation and mindfulness. Presumably teachers that use forms of meditation within classrooms do so with a view to improving the students' relation to something, perhaps their relation to themselves, which may also bring about some improvement in behaviours and exam results. Such efforts to influence could be quite transformative and its use may also be controversial among some parents, though, of course, parental concerns are not decisive particularly where the outcomes for the child are demonstrably good. The problem here is again that education studies is a *human science* in which outcomes are seldom decisively demonstrable. In summary, forms of educational influence vary a great deal, are hard to categorise, and their effects hard to determine. Thus, Education Studies remains a speculative activity, a human science, or as Gert Biesta has called it, a hermeneutic science (Biesta 2011).

6   Religion and Education: the Question of Autonomy

Because forms of influence are central to the concept of education but are so wide and varied as we have just seen, theorists have sought to define a broader educational aim that any kind of influence can be measured against. This foundational aim of all (liberal) education has many names: education for freedom, the formation of reason, rationality or critical thinking, though I have already referred to one particular form of this: 'education for autonomy.' Whatever influences people undergo, those influences should not, so this reasoning generally goes, undermine or restrict their future autonomy (Brighouse, 2006; Clayton, 2006). Indeed, any educational influence should, in the end, establish or enhance the autonomy of the child. The issue of religious influence has been controversial when it has been seen as a force that inhibits or restricts autonomy. We have noted the liberal view that because children are not (yet) autonomous, parents and teachers are justified in seeking to shape their attitudes, beliefs and behaviours as long as, firstly, this kind of influence is in the interests of the child, and secondly, it does not undermine the child's future capacity for autonomy (Giesinger, 2013). This leaves some other key questions to address: First, does religion inhibit autonomy? Second, even if it does, should autonomy be the standard against which all forms of education are measured?

Although the question of whether religion inhibits or enhances autonomy is partly empirical in nature,[6] it also hinges again on what we include in the concept of religion. There are well-known formulations of religion that emphasise its social function. From Durkheim's classic formulation of religion as a fundamental social institution (Durkheim, 1926), the idea of social cohesion has made a comeback given the clash of (religious) cultures that had re-emerged as an issue in recent decades (Huntington, 2002). The etymology of religion 'religare' refers to binding to some kind of obligation, an obligation that has a social character and function. The bonds of religious identity are often connected to community, family and society and entail practices and views that emphasise what we share in common with others. The kinds of

---

6   One ought to recognise that the presence or absence of autonomy is hard to measure empirically and so we should acknowledge that really we are talking about the 'lived experience' of autonomy. A fuller discussion is beyond my scope.

faith commitment that religions encourage, in other words, do not appear to foreground autonomy. Put radically this led to Paul Hirst's accusation that the whole idea of a Christian education is a kind of nonsense (Hirst, 1974), a view that has sparked considerable debate (see, for instance, Cooling, 2010; Shortt, 2018). This view was a logical consequence of the conception of education that emerged in British society at that time: that education ought to be directed towards the formation of universal and shared rationality. Hirst believed that such a view of education was logically inconsistent with the biased influences of Christian education. The formation of reason moves towards a universal and shared rationality in contrast to the particular interests and tendencies of a Christian education. The implication is that the word *education* ought not to be used, but rather it should be replaced with instruction, indoctrination, or evangelisation. Thus, religion can be said to inhibit autonomy. Any influences that sought to secure children's *uncritical* assent to absolute and exclusivist claims would certainly be in contradiction with the general aims of autonomy. But, as the preceding discussion of a pluralist view of religion suggests, this is not the only way of interpreting the lived experience of religious people.

Even if we did establish that religious influence (either religious upbringing or Religious Education) inhibits autonomy, this only justifies the prohibition of such influence if we can also establish that facilitating autonomy should be the primary aim of education. While autonomy may be considered educationally important, is it so clear that any other aim ought to be directed by it? The Catholic parents who wish to raise their children in the Catholic faith may be motivated by the belief that the protection of their child's immortal soul is more important than certain concepts of freedom, rights and autonomy. This kind of argument has its place but seems awkwardly exposed to the charge that it seeks to bring about closed-mindedness in the child (Wareham, 2017). Several liberal theorists argue that secular schools are preferable over religious schools in relation to the development of autonomy (Gardner, 1988; Levinson, 1999). Harry Brighouse has explored similar arguments, but develops a different view arguing that often religious schools are at least as autonomy facilitating as their secular alternatives. He argues that secular schools in America contribute not only to restriction on autonomy, but also to a polarised view of religion along with a general illiteracy concerning religion (Brighouse, 2006). But this becomes an empirical question: to what extent do certain kinds of schools inhibit autonomy? Philosophers are not entirely disengaged from the empirical questions raised here, but the primary form of analysis for philosophers tends to be theoretical. So, in principle, can we acknowledge forms of (religious) influence that do not result in closing the person off from other forms of life?

I do not wish to argue against autonomy as a legitimate educational aim, but my purpose is rather to complicate this view of autonomy. Autonomy could be seen as instrumental or an intrinsic good. Brighouse sees autonomy as instrumentally good since it serves human flourishing (Brighouse 2006). This raises complications with respect to how (and on whose terms) human flourishing is determined, though my more substantial objection is with the idea that autonomy is an intrinsic educational good.

Obviously, there are many ways in which the freedom of little children is restricted for the sake of their safety and their education. For instance, the freedom of toddlers to run around is restricted by parents who know better about the effects of traffic. A child may express their autonomy by choosing to spend the day in their pyjamas while watching cartoons and eating popcorn. The parent who decides to restrict the child's freedom by refusing access to such lifestyle choices exercises educational influence in a way that most liberal theorists accept: this kind of paternalism can enhance future autonomy. The idea that education is fundamentally about the formation of autonomy suffers from a larger conceptual problem, however: the idea of bringing about autonomy entails a contradiction.

The idea that someone should submit or postpone their autonomy for the promise of future autonomy has seemed to theorists of education as inherently contradictory (Giesinger, 2010), a contradiction that goes back to Kant's paradigmatic formulation: "[o]ne of the greatest problems of education is how to unite submission to the necessary restraint with the child's capability of exercising his freewill—for restraint is necessary. How am I to develop the sense of freedom in spite of the restraint?" (Kant 2003, 27). Jacques Rancière has argued that while education appears to concern itself with independence, it does, in fact, produce the precise opposite by making dependency the precondition for a movement towards a putative independence that is never, in fact, accomplished (Rancière, 1991). The path to autonomy is one of submission to another, a submission that is never finally overturned. Rancière's answer to this is that we must assume the presence of equality and autonomy and *practice* these assumptions: acting *as if* they were true. Whatever one makes of Rancière's influential argument (Bingham, Biesta, & Rancière, 2010), it is notable that, in principle, autonomy seems to be something that cannot be the direct result of causal actions of another. This problem might be understood as a form of the general contradiction at the heart of all education, going back to Plato's *Meno*: that learning anything at all depends upon already having the knowledge that one appears to 'learn.'

A common response to the paradox in the *Meno* is that knowing something is never a binary condition: learning is a process of interpreting ideas already partially formed (Aldridge, 2015, pp. 82–83). Just as knowing is not a straight-forward idea, so action and agency are obscure, particularly when we wish to speak of autonomous agents engaged in free action. This indicates something of the complexity surrounding the concept of autonomy, a concept that has surely never existed in its idealised Kantian sense of a wholly responsible subject exercising freedom of the will. That Kantian ideal is bound to fall foul of the complexities of influence, since all sorts of influences, conditions, constraints and 'nudges' can affect the free expression of the pure subjective will, as modern theories of 'choice architecture' have begun to show (Thaler and Sunstein 2008). This work provides a rich seam for future research around the nature of influence with respect to religion.

I have argued that the kinds of influence that we call religious are not fundamentally different from other kinds of influence. The restricted conditions in which 'freedom' is exercised means that forms of influence, even those which affect us in comprehensive matters such as religious forms of life, help to make decisions possible rather than impossible. But if we admit this, must we not also admit that it is not clear what is meant by a free or autonomous decision? I believe this is where we are; in a position that leads to what could be called the 'hermeneutic conditions' of religious influence (Aldridge, 2015). These hermeneutic conditions concern two important restrictions: first, how far our actions and choices are our own, or are formed by the conditions in which freedom exists; and second, how far our influences upon the actions and choices of others are justified for the fulfilment of their own freedom. What should be clear, however, is that influence is not just an unavoidable feature of education, but is also the condition in which freedom as such becomes possible.

7   Conclusion

Interactions between R&E are more frequent, ongoing, deep-rooted and complex than debates about indoctrination and competing rights make us inclined or even able to see.

My argument that the terms of debate have been shaped by certain constructions of R&E is intended to show that there are other ways of thinking about the relations between R&E, and the general concept of influence could be helpful in rethinking these interactions. Influence is a hugely complex and ubiquitous feature of social life, and whether it helps to call these influences *religious* deserves analysis. Following such analysis, we would then be in a better position to see in what ways these influences may, or may not, be justified.

My analysis is not free from assumptions and the debates I have highlighted above can only be taken as one interpretation of a complex and wide-ranging field. My prejudices become more visible where I suggest that the justifications of (religious) influence should be guided by a concern to contribute to what could be called the *lived experience of human freedom*. My comments about the complications of education for autonomy mean that this idea of human freedom requires its own analysis, one of many projects that I hope to see developed in future issues of this journal.

Sociological Perspectives on Religion and Education

Jenny Berglund

Nearly one hundred years ago John Dewey noted that:

> Education in the largest sense is any act or experience that has a forma-
> tive effect on the mind, character, or physical ability of an individual. In
> its technical sense, education is the process by which society deliberately
> transmits its accumulated knowledge, skills and values from one genera-
> tion to another.[1]

From this it can be understood that all state educational systems carry the
potential of being institutions of "indoctrination". Education is the means by
which a state creates what Benedict Anderson so elegantly calls an "imagined
community" (Anderson 1991). Of course, education might conceivably have
more important goals than this. But it is undeniable that throughout the world
attempts are made to instil certain common attitudes, values and ways of
thinking by means of education (Lundén 2011). Until the end of the 19th century, the fostering of good Christians was the principal aim of European school
systems; in the 20th and 21st centuries, their foremost goal has become the
fostering of good citizens. Yet, as worthy as this goal might be, it is obviously
not education's only function. Another is the crucial role that education plays
in the maintenance, preservation, and survival of religious systems. Indeed,
it would not be overstating it to say that education is the indispensable life-
blood of all religious traditions. For members of a majority religion, the transmission of religious traditions to future generations differs from that of those
belonging to a minority religion. Majority society is, in one way or another,
"marinated" in the majority religion. Hence, certain religious values and narratives are transmitted through state institutions, traditions, cultural expressions, and so on—although formal education is also necessary for long-term
survival (Berglund 2013). For minorities, on the other hand, the opportunity to
teach their religion to future generations is far more urgent: if not somehow
conveyed to the young, the religion will eventually disappear.

---

1   John Dewey, *Democracy and Education*. New York: The Free Press, [1916] (1944).

Embedded within the content of this short introductory paragraph are long-standing issues that are of particular concern to sociologists of religion and education, indicating that whether or not they explicitly acknowledge it, in terms of both their interests and their methods, many of those that study religious education are sociologists in practice, having adopted a sociological perspective relative to their work. Indeed, as will be shown below, three of sociology's most prominent founders were, from the start, keenly interested in both religion and education, as well as the interplay between these vital institutions and society as a whole. We begin our examination with a brief historical and definitional overview.

1   Historical and Definitional Overview: Sociology Defined

The Encyclopaedia Britannica informs us that sociology is the study of "human societies, their interactions, and the processes that preserve and change them." The sociologist is said to pursue this objective by examining societal elements such as "institutions, communities, populations, and gender, racial, or age groups" as well as features like social status, social movements, and social change. Britannica further highlights the important role played by social organizations in informing human action, noting that sociology's task is to discover how organizational structures like religious, educational, and political institutions develop, interact, and influence human behaviour. While psychologists are largely interested in studying the individual's internal life or mental sphere, sociologists are primarily concerned with the collective aspects of human behaviour and the ways in which the individual is affected by external structures and groups.

The field of sociology is said to have emerged as a distinct discipline in the mid-1800s as a consequence of Western Europe's scientific, technological and industrial revolutions, which gradually upended traditional societal structures and demanded the development of a more rigorous, scientific means of examining and analysing the social world. While Auguste Comte (1798–1857) and Herbert Spencer (1820–1903) are often regarded as the founder and second-founder of sociology respectively, perhaps the three most influential of the discipline's early contributors were Emile Durkheim (1858–1917), Max Weber (1864–1920), and Karl Marx (1818–1883). The works of all three are considered to have been seminally important to both the sociology of religion and the sociology of education, and their influence continues to resonate in these sub-disciplines even today.

2   What Does It Mean to Adopt a Sociological Perspective?

Peter Berger (1963) once wrote that "the first wisdom of sociology is this—things are not what they seem." In a nutshell, this statement encompasses what it means to adopt a sociological perspective. The fundamental insight of sociology is that our thoughts, attitudes and conduct are in large measure shaped by our sociocultural milieu—i.e., by the social institutions and groups to which we belong as well as the greater society that embeds us, organizing and directing our behaviour. The sociological perspective encourages the application of scientific methods in an attempt to examine the broader social contexts that underlie our actions. It invites us, in other words, to pull back the curtain on social surroundings that we often take for granted—to look beneath the surface of our social world so as to observe those surroundings and their interactions with fresh, more objective and thoroughgoing eyes, thus making the familiar strange and the strange familiar.

3   Sociology of Religion

Sociology of religion employs the tools and methods of the social sciences in the examination of unified systems of beliefs, practices, and values that relate to sacred or spiritual concerns; it also examines the manner in which those systems organize and interact with society as a whole. Sociologists in this area of study are interested in all aspects of religion, including its modes of worship, its expressions in daily life, its relation to secular state interests, its impact on issues of race, gender and sexuality, its diasporic expressions and the challenges that arise therefrom, etc. The concerns of the discipline are not with the validity of this or that religious belief system, but rather with the impact of those systems on both the individual practitioner and society at large. Sociologists are also concerned with the function of religion in both the public and the private sphere, as well as the balance that is struck between the two.

In the wake of 19th century European industrialization and secularization, Durkheim, Weber and Marx recognized the centrality of religion to society, and thus set out to make a scientific examination of the relationship between the two. Indeed, the modern academic study of religion is said to have begun with Durkheim, who considered religion to be an important expression of social cohesion that galvanized the community and bound society's members to the group.

In *Elementary Forms of the Religious Life* (1915), Durkheim argues that "religion happens" in society when there is a separation between the profane and the sacred; the individual perceives a force that transcends self, and then endows that force with supernatural attributes when, "in reality", it is merely our collective social life. For Durkheim, religious ritual, worship, and belief in the supernatural "excite, maintain and recreate certain mental states" that bring people together, provide symbolic focus, and foster social solidarity (Durkheim 1915). Thus, setting aside the matter of God's existence, Durkheim's aim was to understand how religion operates socially in society—an undertaking that has become the basis of sociology's functionalist school of thought.

In contrast to Durkheim, who viewed religion as a stabilizing societal force, Weber considered religion to be distinct from society and a potential stimulator of social change. In studying the impact of religious beliefs on national economies, Weber observed an apparent connection between Protestantism and the rise of capitalism, and in *The Protestant Work Ethic and the Spirit of Capitalism* (1905) he attributed that connection to the fact that Calvinistic thinking had overturned traditional anti-materialist Christian values and replaced them with a rational discipline and work ethic that aided the development of capitalism in certain Northern European countries (Weber 1905).

As to Marx, he clearly rejected the supernatural claims of traditional theologies, maintaining that human beings had invented God in their own image and that the worship of God diverts us from delighting in our own power. For Marx, religion was a social phenomenon that reflected society's social stratification and could not be understood apart from its ideological role in maintaining the status quo and both perpetuating and obfuscating the inequalities of capitalist societies. In perhaps his most oft quoted statement Marx (1844) notes:

> Religious suffering is, at one and the same time, the expression of real suffering and a protest against real suffering. Religion is the sigh of the oppressed creature, the heart of a heartless world, and the soul of soulless conditions. It is the opium of the people ... The abolition of religion as the illusory happiness of the people is the demand for their real happiness ... The criticism of religion disillusions man, so that he will think, act, and fashion his [own] reality ... Religion is only the illusory Sun which revolves around man as long as he does not revolve around himself.

Marx's social theories continue to influence both the sociology of religion and the sociology of education (see below) and are reflected today in both conflict theory and neo-Marxist sociology, which views religion not as a conserving force, but rather as a force for social change and social revolution (as in Latin America).

4   Sociology of Education

From a sociological perspective, education consists of the deliberate process by which society transmits its accumulated knowledge, skills, values, norms, and systems of belief from one generation to another (Dewey 1944). When this process is formalized and differentiated from other social realms, and when it involves defining roles for both teachers and students, it is said to have acquired institutional status, with "schools" epitomizing this type of formalization.[2] The core insight of the sociology of education is that "the school" is a socially embedded institution that both shapes and is shaped by its social milieu in pivotal ways; schools are primary agents of socialization and allocation, and modern societies have developed powerful ideologies indicating that this should be their primary role (Meyer 1977).

Interestingly, the same three figures that made major contributions to the sociology of religion also have had an enduring impact on the sociology of education. The most influential of these is thought to have been Durkheim, who was primarily interested in the contribution of education to the maintenance of social order. Durkheim considered the institution of education (i.e., the school) to be largely responsible for the socialization of future adults as well as the development of societal consensus and solidarity. His thought is said to have laid the foundation for the modern functionalist educational perspective, which sees schools as serving the ideological aims of the given social order, providing individuals with both cognitive skills and the appropriate cultural outlook, and generating "good" productive citizens (Parsons 1959; Dreeben 1968).

While Weber's early sociological writings did not directly examine education per se, his theory of social structure and the interplay between social class, social status, and power recognized the importance of institutional structures (like schools) through which dominant social groups attempt to maintain their position in society (Collins 1979). Arising out of the Weberian tradition, the status conflict perspective on education emphasizes the attempts of various groups—primarily defined by ethnicity, race, and class—to use education as a mechanism to win or maintain privilege (Collins 1979).

---

2   https://www.encyclopedia.com/social-sciences/encyclopedias-almanacs-transcripts-and -maps/sociology-education.

Although Marx neither worked to integrate education into his theory of capitalism nor focused directly on education in his theory of society, he was nonetheless concerned with the tendency of education to serve the interest of the ruling class in maintaining its social dominance (Bowles and Gintis 1976). His ideas in this regard are reflected in modern neo-Marxist theories of education, which have provided the most thoroughgoing challenge to the functionalist position. Their essential point is that schools are organized to fulfil the needs of capitalism, which are to transfer privilege from generation to generation and to effectively assign differently socialized individuals to their appropriate slots in the corporate hierarchy; as such, "the changing demands of capitalist production and the power of capitalist elites determine the nature of the educational system" (Bowles and Gintis 1976).

As a major contributor to the field of sociology and to the testing of established theories, sociology of education plays an important role in the discipline's continuing development. Durkheim provided a sociological conceptualization of education as a system that transmits society's culture and social order to new generations, and both Marx and Weber have contributed to sociology of education's conceptual and theoretical roots:

> Marx laid down the foundations for conflict theory, and later conflict theorists have explored the ideological role of the state in education as it reproduces and maintains class statuses. Weber developed a multidimensional approach in which structure, human agency, the material and the normative were combined. Building on this early foundation, several more recent directions have emerged. Among structural conflict theories, Pierre Bourdieu's (1984) theory of practice, Basil Bernstein's (1996) theory of language codes and Randall Collins's (1979) Weberian theory of social exclusion have had a major impact on contemporary sociology of education.[3]

Having briefly examined the history and defining features of both sociology of religion and sociology of education, we will now examine how all this applies to the matters of religious education, religious diversity, and religious-teacher education. We also will discuss the methodologies that social scientists employ in the study of such topics.

---

3 A. Gary Dworkin, et al: *The Sociology of Education* (January, 2013) at https://www.researchgate.net/publication/323953531_The_sociology_of_education.

5   The Study of Religious Education, Religious Diversity, and Teacher
        Education

Before beginning this discussion, it is important to note that many of the issues
raised by functional, conflict, and neo-Marxist theorist in both the sociology of
religion and the sociology of education are (with necessary adjustments) also
of concern to researchers that study such matters as minority religious education, state funding of religious education, confessional vs non-confessional
religious education, the influence of the teacher on religious schooling, the
impact of religious and cultural diversity in mainstream schools, the experiences of minority children and their parents in the secular school system,
and so on.

In many countries, the study of religious education has emerged from the
pedagogical and spiritual needs of religious communities to convey their traditions to future generations. In such cases, the study of religious education
has been a largely normative theological discipline, meaning that its primary
aim has been to more effectively shape and maintain the traditional religious
thinking of younger generations. Social science scholars also have displayed
an abiding interest in the study of religious education, not because of a desire
to increase the religiosity of a given youth population, but rather because it is
an intriguing field that provides valuable insight into the relation between religion, education, and society. Apart from the general issues mentioned above,
some of the questions that researchers of religious education seek to explore
are as follows: how students that partake of religious education register that
experience; why certain religious voices and practices are silenced or discour-
aged in mainstream schools; how mass media affects the teaching of religious
education; why parents choose to place their children in faith-based rather
than secular schools; how religious education operates as a social structure
that influences students' decisions and actions, and so on.

This leads to another important aspect of the sociology of R&E: the study
of the interplay between the individual and the social structures in which she/
he is embedded.[4] Here it is important to note that while some social structures are obvious and discernible, others are largely indiscernible, although
their impact is often just as profound. A school, for example, constitutes a
discernible social structure in the sense that it is an overt means by which
a state (or organization) attempts to socializes its citizens (or members) in a

---

4   I use social orders in a wide way, and include both rather solidified societal structures and
    more dynamic patterns in social relations. The impact is mutual.

particular way. And yet within that overt structure, there are covert aspects that can exert either a positive or a negative influence relative to that social-izing process—e.g., teacher attitudes, textbooks, curricula choices, sources of funding, and so forth. Moreover, that which is considered acceptable and unacceptable in schools is often indiscernible, although the subtle signals of these covert influences can be as determinative as the lines in a stone.

For example, the stated aim of the Swedish school system is to be non-denominational, objective and neutral in the matter of religious preference. Yet, after conducting fieldwork in Swedish religious education classrooms for three months, a colleague from the Czech Republic remarked that rather than encountering the "neutral" religious education environment she had expect-ed, she had encountered the "Mecca of Lutheranism" instead: adherence to the Protestant Lutheran calendar, school celebrations of Protestant Lutheran holidays, a teaching staff with little or no knowledge of non-Christian holi-days, textbooks that presented alternate-Christian and non-Christian reli-gions in a negative light, Protestantism viewed as reflecting liberal democratic values, with other religions viewed as having a more authoritarian style, etc. She also observed that all this seemed to be occurring "below the radar", with-out the slightest recognition that the educational system's proclaimed non-denominationalism, objectivity, and neutrality had been compromised. Here it should be noted that I was not at all taken aback by her assessment, since I have noticed this anomaly in my own fieldwork and had received similar ac-counts from many others over the years.

Elsewhere I have described this phenomenon as being comparable to the process of marination, whereby food is soaked in a seasoned liquid that per-manently alters its flavour and cannot be washed away. While one must be cautious about making broad generalizations, it is a fact that Sweden's ma-jority institutions (including its educational institution) had marinated in the Protestant Lutheran tradition for many centuries before attempts were made to reduce Christian emphases and secularize Swedish schools. Finally, in 1962 it was officially stipulated that religious education should be non-denominational, meaning more neutral, secular, and objective in the matter of religion. However, like cooking marinades, marinades of culture, history and language penetrate deeply into the marrow of a society; thus even when well-intended attempts are made to "wash them away", their "flavour" con-tinues to permeate below the surface, not having been entirely expunged. One recommended method of dealing with such situations is to bring the matter to conscious awareness through self-reflection, and then to recog-nize and adjust for the "marinade's" presence in the daily functioning of Swedish schools.

6   Quantitative vs Qualitative Research Methods

Social science researchers employ both quantitative and qualitative methods in the exploration of their various research questions. Both methods have their advantages and disadvantages, yet certain researchers clearly prefer the one over the other, largely depending on the types of questions they are interested in asking. Suppose a researcher desires to study Islamic religious education. There are many possible ways of approaching this topic and a large variety of questions that could be asked. A given researcher, for example, may want to know how mosque attendance among young Muslim adults is affected by the receipt of Islamic religious education. To answer this question, the researcher might collect data on the two variables—mosque attendance by young Muslim adults and Islamic religious education—to see if there is a statistical correlation between them. If it turns out that there is a strong positive correlation, we can then assert that Islamic religious education is to some degree predictive of mosque attendance among young Muslim adults. Yet another researcher may have a very different question in mind; she may want to examine, for example, what Islamic religious education has *meant* to young Muslim adults. To properly investigate this question, however, will require an intimate knowledge of the experiences, impressions and retrospective reflections of those adults. Thus, while the collection of data on Islamic religious education may enable the prediction of mosque attendance among young Muslim adults, knowing what Islamic religious education has meant to those adults requires a deeper understanding of who they are and how they view that experience. While quantitative methods are well suited in terms of answering the former question, qualitative methods are far more appropriate in terms addressing the latter one.

7   The Quantitative Approach

In *The Practice of Social Research* (2010), Earl Babbie describes the quantitative approach as follows:

> Quantitative methods consist of objective measurements and the statistical, mathematical, or numerical analysis of data collected through polls, questionnaires, and surveys, or by manipulating pre-existing statistical data using computational techniques. Quantitative research focuses on gathering numerical data and generalizing it across groups of people or to explain a particular phenomenon.

Such methods are said to provide a more objective, scientific means of researching a problem, in which data is gathered, controlled, and measured using structured research instruments and results are based on large sample sizes that are considered representative of a given population. Thus, while the results of quantitative research may be "statistically" significant, they are less likely to be "humanly" significant (Babbie 2010).

Approaching social scientific questions quantitatively allows for broader studies, the results of which are thought to be more objective, accurate and readily generalisable; moreover, quantitative methods tend to be less influenced by the personal biases of the researcher and more capable of being replicated and compared to other studies. On the downside, such methods sometimes miss contextual detail, provide numerical descriptions rather than detailed narratives, afford less information about behaviour, attitudes and motivations, and call for the development of standardized questions that are susceptible to structural bias and false representations. Thus, while quantitative methods may be suitable for understanding the diffusiveness and/or commonness of a given phenomenon, they tend to remain superficial and fragmentary.

8   The Qualitative Approach

Among the various approaches that reside under the umbrella of qualitative research—e.g., narrative, phenomenology, grounded theory, historical research, content analysis, etc.—the ethnographic approach seems the one most preferred by social scientists that explore religious education and related topics. This is because an ethnographic approach—which involves qualitative methods such as participant observations, in-depth interviews, case studies, open-ended responses, and fieldnotes—enables the researcher to explore the features, attributes, and subtleties of a given social phenomenon, thus yielding material of a more rich and comprehensive nature. The qualitative approach is generally employed by researchers that are interested in deeply studying, describing, and interpreting the behaviour, values, meanings, and interactions of members of a given group:

> Researchers that employ qualitative methods emphasize the value-laden nature of inquiry. They seek answers to questions that stress how social experience is created and given meaning. In general, qualitative researchers attempt to describe and interpret human behavior based primarily on the words of selected individuals ... and/or through the interpretation of their material culture or occupied space. There is a reflexive process

underpinning every stage of a qualitative study to ensure that researcher biases, presuppositions, and interpretations are clearly evident, thus
ensuring that the reader is better able to interpret the overall validity of
the research.[5]

Qualitative research generates detailed data, responds to local situations and
participant needs, provides multiple contexts of understanding, interacts with
participants on their own terms, creates a descriptive capability based on
primary and unstructured data, attempts to leave the perspective of participants intact, and aims to afford a holistic view of a given phenomenon. On the
downside, qualitative studies are often more expensive and time consuming,
less generalisable, more difficult to replicate, more apt to encounter ethical
dilemmas that can undermine overall validity, less capable of investigating and
establishing causal links, and more prone to subjective bias in the collection,
interpretation and reporting of data. Moreover, the qualitative study of religious education among minorities can pose special challenges when it comes
to gaining access and trust.

9   Quantitative Studies

The primary aim of the EU-funded REDCo-project[6] was to "explore and com-
pare the potentials and limitations of religion in the educational systems of
selected European countries" in order to discover ways in which religious education might be used to promote dialogue and mutual respect in the context
of European development and identity formation (Weiss 2010). In one aspect
of this study, which examined student attitudes toward religious diversity, researchers carried out a standardized quantitative survey (based upon a previously held qualitative study) that included a total number of 8,000+ students
in the 14 to 16-year age group. The samples were not intended to be statistically representative, but rather were designed to reflect regional or national
contexts by applying certain criteria to the process of selecting participating
schools; some national samples, moreover, were intentionally concentrated on
specific regions.

---

5   Denzin, Norman. K. and Yvonna S. Lincoln. "Introduction: The Discipline and Practice of
    Qualitative Research." In *The Sage Handbook of Qualitative Research*. Norman. K. Denzin and
    Yvonna S. Lincoln, eds. 3rd edition. (Thousand Oaks, CA: Sage, 2005), p. 10.
6   Wolfram Weisse (2010) REDCo: A European Research Project on Religion in Education,
    Religion & Education, 37:3, 187–202, DOI: 10.1080/15507394.2010.513937.

After subjecting their findings to statistical analysis, the study's researchers drew the following general conclusions with regard to teen-age attitudes toward religious heterogeneity:

1. Religious pluralism is not only accepted, but widely welcomed. The majority believe that people of different religions can live together in harmony.

2. The responding pupils are critical of truth claims that exclude people of different beliefs or faiths.

3. Although pupils are clearly aware of the conflict potential of religion and religious plurality, the majority of young people share a vision of peaceful coexistence in a religiously plural Europe. The realisation of this vision is often presented as contingent on the existence of attitudes of tolerance, open-mindedness and respect, and on the exercise of key dialogue skills: learning about each other's beliefs; listening to each other; getting to know a variety of views.[7]

Researchers noted that the beliefs and thoughts expressed by their respondents were "quite remarkable", displaying an immense openness toward religious and societal pluralism as well as an awareness of the importance of dialogue in the realization of "peaceful coexistence in European societies (Weiss 2010, pp. 196)."

10   Qualitative Studies

As previously noted, qualitative research on religious education is often based on various types of ethnographic studies, many of which involve interviews and participant observations.[8] In the *Oxford Handbook of the Sociology of Religion* (2011), Eleanor Nesbitt divides teachers of religion into two categories: those that are committed "to particular interpretations of particular faiths"; and those that are "scholars professionally engaged in theology or the social

---

7   Weiss 2010, pp. 196

8   Green and Bloome distinguish between at least two different approaches pertaining to ethnography and the field of education: ethnographic studies *of* and *in* education. When a study is guided by educational questions and concerns, it is primarily an ethnographic study *in* education, although it borrows from the ethnography *of* education as well. An ethnographic study *of* education focuses on the educational setting as a place of inquiry and involves anthropologists and sociologists that use their disciplines' theoretical frameworks, tools of inquiry, etc. to construct an understanding of what counts as education to a local group (Green & Bloome 1996:187). According to Walford 2007:vii, ethnography has become one of the primary methods of researching educational settings. This also applies to the study of religious education (see also Nesbitt 2004).

sciences".[9] Nesbitt then proposes that both types of religious teachers can avoid stereotyping and other pitfalls in the teaching of religion by becoming ethnographically aware, meaning to self-reflectively bring one's own view of religion to conscious awareness—a process that entails challenging the taken-for-granted equation of religion with belief and practice. In addition, teacher observations of the expressions of different religious traditions in the local school context are said to carry the potential of enriching their own teaching of religious education. Thus, teachers that increase their own ethnographic awareness are better able to increase the cultural literacy and openness of the various types of students in their class (see also Berglund 2014; Nesbitt 2004). Nesbitt concludes:

> An ethnographic approach to the teaching and study of religions re-duces the risk of assuming religions to be bounded, static, internally homogeneous, depersonalized entities, and of presenting them in this reified and essentialized way. Instead, both teacher and student engage with the dynamics of individuals in their various interpenetrating group-ings, and their own self-understanding develops through this engage-ment. Boundaries between oneself and others are unsettled, and teacher and student progress together along paths of continuing discovery and relearning.

In the section "Perspectives: Mediatized Religious Education" (2018), Audun Toft and Maximilian Broberg review two of their own qualitative studies (one in Norway and one in Sweden), which utilize participant observations, teacher observations, and semi-structured teacher interviews to better comprehend how media materials and media representations are employed in the peda-gogical practice of teaching and learning about religion. They also examine how these materials and representations affect the teacher's choice of topics and the manner in which she/he presents them. Toft and Broberg explain:

> Mediatization theory states that in modern society, the media are estab-lished as an institution in their own right, and other institutions come to depend on the media in their everyday practices and communication (Schrott 2009; Hjarvard 2013). This may alter institutional practices, as dynamics inherent in the operations of the media thus influence the in-teractions within the said institution ... [Here] we examine how repre-sentations of religion and topics related to religion, in the form of media

---

9   Nesbitt's chapter is named, "The Teacher of Religion as Ethnographer."

discourses and materials produced by and for the mass media, play a role in the lessons observed. We argue that media representations form an integral and consistent part of the practice of religious education as a way to relate the content of the subject to contemporary society. This, however, has some ramifications for how religion is engaged with, as various media dynamics come to influence the classroom practice.[10]

One of the strengths of complementing observational data with interviews is that this affords access to diachronic perspectives. Thus, while observations of classroom teaching provide information about the context in which that teaching occurs, in-depth teacher interviews provide information about how that teaching has changed over time as well as the reasoning that has gone into teachers' pedagogical choices. Post-observational interviews also allow for reflection, dialogue, and deeper discussion on both the teacher's pedagogical choices and the researcher's initial observations.

11   National Comparisons and International Knowledge Transmission

Drawing national comparison of religious education is particularly challenging due inherent between-country differences in both educational systems and religious education across Europe (Oddrun Bråten 2014; 2016). This notwithstanding, working comparatively across national borders can enable the accumulation of a vast amount of empirical data that will advance our understanding of religious education as well as its relation to important educational and societal elements on both a national and an international level. Comparative studies, for example, open numerous possibilities for countries to learn from each other's approach to religious education through the exchange of empirical data and knowledge on matters such as teaching methods, the organization and aims of religious education, the content of religious education textbooks, the comparative experiences of teachers and students operating under different approaches, the effects of religious education on value and citizenship development, and so forth; such studies also can bring to light certain peculiarities of a given country's approach to religious education when that approach is juxtaposed with the approach of other countries (Berglund 2013; Niemi 2016).

Today many European countries face common challenges when it comes to organising religious education in secular schools, securing the rights of minority

---

10   Toft and Broberg 2018, 106.

students in the face of increasing xenophobia, counteracting manifestations of extremism in school, and so on. Meeting these sorts of challenges would certainly be aided by increasing the international transmission of knowledge in the field of religious education. This fact has motivated a diverse group of religious education scholars to hold intensive discussions on the challenge of international knowledge transfer, after which they published a manifesto calling for broader discussions on this topic in different countries as well as in leading religious education periodicals.[11]

In my own between-country studies of Islamic religious education in Europe, I have argued as follows for the social scientific value of comparative studies: 1) empirically, such studies highlight between-country similarities and differences regarding the provision of religious education as well as how various types of faith-based schooling adapt to each nation's educational setting; and, 2) comparative studies of publicly funded minority education can serve as a type of litmus test—or indicator of the broader relationship between various Western democracies and their minority populations (Berglund 2015).

12   Conclusion

Most social scientists would agree that even the most empirically grounded sociological studies, and the understandings derived therefrom, require interpretations of data that are not purely objective, but rather involve degrees of subjective judgement. Acknowledging this, however, is not meant to imply that all interpretations are necessarily of the same value. There are, of course, certain general scientific standards, such as the important demand for a comprehensive presentation of findings in which competing arguments are fairly and accurately represented. Moreover, given the fact that total objectivity is an unattainable ideal—that no researcher can wholly transcend his/her personal background, values, preferences, self-interests, prejudices, and so forth—there is a need for transparency not only in terms of delineating methods, procedures, and research limitations, but also in terms of reflecting upon and explicating the potential impact of one's own personal background and influences on the questions raised, the direction taken, the methods employed, the analysis conducted, and the conclusions drawn therefrom. It must be remembered that researchers are ordinary members of the human

---

11   https://comenius.de/themen/Evangelische-Bildungsverantwortung-in-Europa/2019
        -Manifesto_on-International-Knowledge-Transfer-in-Religious-Education.pdf?m=
        1552893898.

community, with their own religious, political, and personal interpretative frameworks and sympathies. The decision to train one's spotlight onto a given object necessarily means that other objects will remain in the dark. It is well-known, for example, that "ascriptive identity categories" such as gender, age, ethnicity and religious belonging can potentially influence the research situation (Lofland 2006). All of this highlights the importance of backing one's research conclusions with solid data and empirical evidence—with the caveat (already mentioned above) that at some point in the process all empirical material must be subject to interpretation, and that such material can be measured and analysed in very different ways, based upon various subjective choices. It is thus imperative that researchers remain open to revisiting and revising their conclusions in light of the most recent findings.

Conclusion: the Potential of Further Research in Religion and Education

Stephen G. Parker

In this final section, I want to briefly outline some areas ripe for further research in R&E, beyond the focus upon policy, curriculum and pedagogy, which tend to dominate the pages of much of the academic literature. These areas are the historicizing R&E; the sensory, spatial and material aspects of R&E; mission and empire; and children's rights and agency. I conclude by stressing the editorial agenda we hope will shape this new series. Firstly, some brief remarks about some potential areas for further research.

1   Historicizing, Contextualising and Conceptualising Religion and Education and Religious Education

At various points throughout, this first issue of *Religion and Education* has argued that we need to historicize, contextualize and conceptualize R&E and religious education. We have begun to approach the matter here but realise that there is still much to be done. We therefore encourage much more further thinking in this regard.

Contemporary discussion and questions around the subject matter naturally have the tendency for focus upon present-day concerns and problems (Freathy and Parker, 2010). Such discussions are neglectful of the value of querying how these matters have been understood in the past and why (that is exploring history of the ideas and debates in R&E and religious education), and what contexts they were formed within (that is the social, political, cultural and religious history). Too often to this tendency overlooks the value of such knowledge to the empowering of contemporary agency in decision-making, policy action, and curriculum development (Freathy and Parker, 2015).

2   The Sensory, Spatial and Material Aspects of Religion and Education

In an article on the spatial dimensions of education I explored how religious education happens beyond the curriculum, even within the topography of the educational spaces. I argued, that the places set aside for prayer and reflection, the bodily-spatial and physical routines of schooling inscribe children with a sense of self, reinforcing or challenging their religious and cultural identity (Parker, 2009). Such studies of the ways in which children's bodies become the medium through which they are religiously and morally educated is rare (Parker, 2017). Likewise, the emotional, sensory and material dimensions of religion and education are equally neglected (Crutchley, Parker and Roberts, 2019). In Religious Studies, these facets of religious life have received a good deal of attention (for instance on the emotions see Riis and Woodhead 2012; on material culture see Morgan 2009; on the visual see Morgan 2012), but in terms of R&E as a field, there is much more to be done in applying critical theories and methodologies to educational contexts.

3   Mission and Empire

Historically, education has gone hand-in-hand with imperial expansion and parallel Christian missionary activity (as Deirdre Raftery observes in her section), thus problematically in conjunction with colonialization and the exercise of institutional and political power (Vallgårda (2015); Morrison and Martin (2017). Likewise, in many national contexts the churches were the first to establish schools for the masses as part of its mission. In England, for instance, the development of education, which notably included the reading of the Bible, went hand in hand—though not without significant furore and denominational dispute—over the content of a basic religious education (Parker and Freathy, 2019). Cultural and political contingencies affected how (religious) schooling and religious education developed in some societies. Vested interests, layers of power and ideological hegemony have shaped R&E and religious education. Such matters require increased critical focus.

4   Children's Rights and Agency in Religion and Education

Literature in the field of R&E is undoubtedly growing, partly as a result of contemporary questions about how children are socialized across religions, not least due to concerns about the so-called 'radicalization' of children and young people. In this context, the historiography has some interesting parallels and resonances, see for example Lucy Underwood's book Childhood, *Youth and Religious Dissent in Post-Reformation England* (Underwood, 2014), strongly indicating how religions have continually been a means of cultural change and resistance to change, not least amongst the young. How matters of religion and education look from the perspective and experience of children and young people should be a priority area of research. In light of scholarship around the moral meanings given to children and childhood (Lynch, 2014), and the scandals around child abuse in religious contexts (Donnelly, 2017), there is an emerging ethical as well as scholarly imperative to consider how children experience, navigate and respond to the religious, not least in educational contexts (Shillitoe, forthcoming 2020).

5   Religious Education and Developments in Theology and Religious Studies

Despite some alignment between religious education in schools and developments in the discipline of Religious Studies in universities, there has been surprisingly little academic dialogue between these disciplines, in the English context at least. Yes, Religious Education in schools without a religious character in England gradually moved from being predominantly confessional in mode, and Christianity-focused in content, towards a multi-faith curriculum in the from the 1970s, but scholarship in the burgeoning disciplines of Religious Studies has had little traction and impact upon religious education in the UK. Why is this?

University researchers in religious education have tended to network with other religious educationalists rather than with scholars of religious and theological studies. Thus, the relation between matters of R&E have, on the whole, been predominantly viewed from the perspective of the methodologies serving education rather than those service religious and theological studies. This has led on the whole to a relative disconnection in scholarship between pedagogy on the one hand and the academic subjects of the discipline. Within-university collaborations between religious educationalists and researchers in Theology and Religious Studies has been relatively rare. How might developments in Theology and Religious Studies, and the critical theories deployed in these fields, be utilised to inform studies of R&E? With the publication of this journal it is hoped that the balance will shift the other way towards a richer dialogue between those working at the poles of the intersection between R&E, and that this intersection is viewed as much from the religion side of things as the educational.

6   Conclusion: Achieving Cross-/Inter-disciplinary Perspectives

The *Religion and Education* is intended to represent multi-disciplinary perspectives with the goal of generating cross- and inter-disciplinary insights.
Readers of this new journal will be wondering whether and how such cross-
and inter-disciplinary ambitions might be achieved. Firstly, I see the responsibility for this being upon both the editors and authors. It is our editorial goal
to ensure that there is a balance of disciplinary perspectives is represented
with the journal. In particular, commissioning issues of the journal in areas
of the neglected historical and philosophical dimensions to the study of
R&E will be a priority, because such studies have the potential to add depth
of understanding to the lengthy trajectory of many contemporary issues and
problems. Moreover, I see it as a responsibility of authors to draw upon, and
draw out, the cross- and inter-disciplinary perspectives in their contributions to
the journal. Where published studies give priority to particular methodological
perspectives, authors need to ask themselves what historical, theoretical or
empirical studies might contribute to their work. Drawing these out for the
reader is an authorial responsibility, and thankfully the lengthier nature of
issues in the *Religion and Education* makes such observations possible.

Bibliography

Afdal, G. 2008. 'Religious education as a research discipline: an activity theoretical perspective'. *British Journal of Religious Education*. 30:3, 199–210.

Aldridge, D. 2011. 'What is religious education all about? A hermeneutic reappraisal'. *Journal of Beliefs & Values*, 32: 1, 33–45.

Aldridge, D. 2015. *A hermeneutics of religious education*. London/New York: Bloomsbury.

Aldridge, D. 2018. 'Religious Education's Double Hermeneutic'. *British Journal of Religious Education*, 40: 3, 245–256.

Allen, J. 2008. 'Slavery, colonialism and the pursuit of community life: Anglican mission education in Zanzibar and Northern Rhodesia, 1864–1940'. *History of Education*, 37:2, 207–226.

Allender, T. 2003. 'Anglican evangelism in North India and the Punjabi missionary classroom: the failure to educate "the masses", 1860–77'. *History of Education*, 32:3, 273–288.

Allender, T. 2010. 'Understanding education and India: new turns in postcolonial scholarship'. *History of Education*, 39:2, 281–288.

Allender, T. 2016. *Learning Femininity in Colonial India, 1820–1932*. Manchester: Manchester University Press.

Allender, T. 2017. 'Household *bibis*, pious learning and racial cure: changing feminine identities in colonial India, 1780–1925'. *Paedagogica Historica*, 53:1–2, 155–169.

Anderson, B. 1991. *Imagined Communities: Reflections on the Origin and Spread of Nationalism*. London and New York: Verso.

Anderson, Gerald *et al*, (eds). 1994. *Mission Legacies: Biographical Studies of Leaders of the Modern Missionary Movement*. New York: Orbis Books, 1994.

Anon. 1961. *Joyful Mother of Children: Mother Frances Mary Teresa Ball, by a Loreto Sister* IBVM. Dublin: Gill & Macmillan.

Archibald, G. H. 1926. *The Modern Sunday School: its psychology and methods*. London: Pilgrim Press.

Arthur, J. 2019. 'Christianity and the character education movement, 1897–1914'. *History of Education*, 48:1, 60–76.

Asad, T. 2003. *Formations of the secular: Christianity, Islam, modernity*. Stanford, California: Stanford University Press.

Avest, I. 2012. *On the Edge: (Auto)biography and Pedagogical Theories on Religious Education*. Rotterdam: Sense Publishers.

Babbie, E. R. 2010. *The Practice of Social Research*. 12th ed. Belmont. CA: Wadsworth Cengage.

Bara, J. 2005. 'Seeds of mistrust: tribal and colonial perspectives on education in Chotanagpur, 1834–c. 1850'. *History of Education*, 34:6, 617–637.

Barbour, I. G. 1998. *Religion and science: historical and contemporary issues.* London: SCM.

Barnes, L. P. 2008. 'Michael Hand, Is Religious Education Possible?'. *Studies in Philosophy and Education,* 27:1, 63–70.

Barnes, L. P. 2011. 'Religious Education: Taking religious difference seriously'. *Impact,* 17, New Jersey: Wiley Blackwell.

Barnes, L. P., and Wright, A. 2006. 'Romanticism, representations of religion and critical religious education'. *British Journal of Religious Education,* 28:1, 65–77.

Bartle, G. F. 1994. 'The role of the British and Foreign School Society in elementary education in India and the East Indies, 1813–75'. *History of Education,* 23:1, 17–33.

Bell, C. 2006. 'Paradigms behind (and before) the modern concept of religion', *History and Theory* 45: December, 27–46.

Bellaigue, C. de. 2004. 'Behind the School Walls: the School Community in French and English Boarding Schools for Girls, 1810–1867'. *Paedagogica Historica,* 40:1–2, 107–121.

Bellenoit, H. 2007. *Missionary Education and Empire in Late Colonial India, 1860–1920.* London: Pickering and Chatto.

Berger, P. L. 1963. *Invitation to Sociology. A Humanistic Perspective.* New York: Anchor Books, Doubleday & Company, Inc.

Berglund, J. 2010. *Teaching Islam, Islamic Religious Education in Sweden.* Münster: Waxmann.

Berglund, J. 2013. 'Swedish religion education—Objective but Marinated in Lutheran Protestantism?' *Temenos,* 49:2, 165–184.

Berglund, J. 2014. 'An ethnographic eye on religion in everyday life'. *British Journal of Religious Education.* 36:1, 39–52.

Berglund, J. 2015. *Publicly funded Islamic Education in Europe and the United States.* Washington: The Brookings Institution.

Berglund, J. 2016. 'Islamic Religious Education in Muslim Schools: A Translation of Islam to the Swedish School System'. In Berglund, J., Schanneik, Y., Bocking, B. (eds). *Religious Education in Global and Local World.* London: Springer.

Berglund, J. 2017. 'The Study of Islamic Education, A Litmus Test on State Relations to Muslim Minorities'. Fuhrding, S. ed. *Method and Theory in the Study of Religions.* The Netherlands: Brill Academic Publishers, 232–258.

Berglund, J. ed. (2018). *European Perspectives on Islamic Education and Public Schooling.* Equinox.

Berglund, J. 2018. 'Islamundervisning i det oförutsägbara klassrummet'. In Franck, O. and Thalén, P. *Interkulturell religionsdidaktik: Utmaningar och möjligheter.* red. Lund: Studentlitteratur.

Bertram-Troost, G. D., De Roos, S. A., & Miedema, S. 2006. 'Religious identity development of adolescents in religiously affiliated schools: A theoretical foundation for empirical research'. *Journal of Beliefs and Values,* 27:3, 303–314.

Biesta, G. 2010. *Good education in an age of measurement: ethics, politics, democracy.* Boulder, Colo. London: Paradigm.

Biesta, G. 2011. Disciplines and theory in the academic study of education: a comparative analysis of the Anglo-American and Continental construction of the field. *Pedagogy, Culture & Society,* 19:2, 175–192.

Billington, R. 2002. *Religion without God.* London: Routledge.

Bingham, C. W., Biesta, G., and Rancière, J. 2010. *Jacques Rancière: education, truth, emancipation.* London/New York: Continuum.

Blinkova, A., & Vermeer, P. 2018. Religious education in Russia: a comparative and critical analysis, *British Journal of Religious Education,* 40:2, 194–206.

Borell, K. and Gerdner, A. 2011. 'Hidden Voluntary Social Work: A Nationally Representative Survey of Muslim Congregations in Sweden'. *British Journal of Social Work.* 41, 968–979.

Bowden, C. 1999. '"For the glory of God": a study of the education of English Catholic women in convents in Flanders and France in the first half of the seventeenth century'. *Paedagogica Historica,* Supplementary Series V. Ghent: CSHP.

Bowden, C. 2005. 'Community space and cultural transmission: formation and schooling in English enclosed convents in the seventeenth century'. *History of Education,* 34:4, 365–386.

Bowie, F., Kirkwood, D. and Ardener, S. 1993. *Women and Missions: Past and Present, Anthropological and Historical Perceptions.* Oxford and RI: Berg.

Bowles, S. and Gintis, H. 1976. *Schooling in Capitalist America: Educational Reform and the Contradictions of Economic Life.* New York: Basic Books.

Braten, O. Comparative Perspective on the History of Religious Education: England and Norway. In Parker, S. G., Freathy, R. J. K., Francis, L. J. (2015) *History, Remembrance and Religious Education.* Oxford: Peter Lang.

Bråten, O. 2016. 'Comparative Studies in Religious Education: Perspectives Formed Around a Suggested Methodology'. In (Eds.) Berglund, J. Schanneik, Y. *Religious Education in Global and Local World.* Brian Bocking. Springer.

Bråten, O. M. H. 2014. 'Are oranges the only fruit? A discussion of comparative studies in religious education in relation to the plural nature of the field internationally'. In Rothgangel, M., Skeie, G. and Jäggle, M. eds. *Religious education at schools in Europe.* Vienna: Vienna University Press, 19–43.

Brendon, V. 2006. *Children of the Raj.* London: Phoenix.

Brighouse, H. 2006. *On education.* Abingdon: Routledge.

Browning, D. and Miller-McLemore, B.J. 2009. *Children and Childhood in American Religions.* Rutgers: Rutgers University Press.

Bruno-Jofré, R. 2005. *The Missionary Oblate Sisters: Vision and Mission.* Montreal: McGill-Queen's University Press.

Buchardt, M. 2015 'Cultural Protestantism and Nordic Religious Education: An incision in the historical layers behind the Nordic welfare state model'. *Nordidactica— Journal of Humanities and Social Science Education*, 2015: 2, 131–165.

Burley, S. 2005. 'An overview of the historiography of women religious in Australia'. *Journal of the Australian Catholic Historical Society*, 26, 43–60.

Burley, S. 2012. 'Engagement with Empires: Irish Catholic Female Religious Teachers in Colonial South Australia, 1868–1901'. *Irish Educational Studies*, 31, no. 2.

Butler, A. M. 2012. *Across God's Frontiers: Catholic Sisters in the American West, 1850– 1920*. North Carolina: University of North Carolina Press.

Callan, E. and Arena, D. 2010. Indoctrination. In H. Siegel, ed. *The Oxford Handbook of Philosophy of Education*. Oxford: Oxford University Press.

Carmody, B. 1999. 'Catholic schools in Zambia, 1891–1924'. *History of Education*, 28:1, 73–86.

Carmody, B. 2000. 'Zambia's Catholic schools and secularization'. *History of Education*, 29:4, 357–371.

Carmody, B. 2016. 'The Catholic school and social justice in Africa: a Zambian case study'. *Paedagogica Historica*, 52:5, 559–574.

Chan F. N. K. 2015. Religious Education in Hong Kong Catholic Schools: Past, Present and Future. In: Buchanan M., Gellel A. M. eds. *Global Perspectives on Catholic Religious Education in Schools*. Springer, Cham.

Chauduri, N. and Stroebel, M. 1990. 'Western Women and Imperialism'. *Women's Studies International Forum* 8:4.

Chiu, P. 2008. '"A position of usefulness": in colonial Hong Kong (1850s–1890s)', *History of Education*, 37:6, 789–805.

Chryssides, G. and Zeller, B. 2016. *The Bloomsbury Companions to New Religious Movements*. London: Bloomsbury.

Church of England, 2016. *Church of England Vision for Education: Deeply Christian, serving the common good*. London: Church of England Education Office. https:// www.churchofengland.org/sites/default/files/2017-10/2016%20Church%20 of%20England%20Vision%20for%20Education%20WEB%20FINAL.pdf (accessed February 2019).

Clark, E. 2007. *'Masterless Mistresses: the New Orleans Ursulines and the Development of a New World Society, 1727–1884'*. Chapel Hill: University of North Carolina Press.

Clayton, M. 2006. *Justice and legitimacy in upbringing*. Oxford: Oxford University Press.

Clayton, M., 2012. 'Debate: The Case against the Comprehensive Enrolment of Children'. *Journal of Political Philosophy*, 20, 353–364.

Clayton, M., Mason, A., Swift, A., and Wareham, R. 2018. How to regulate faith schools?. *Impact* 25, New Jersey: Wiley Blackwell.

Coburn, C. 2004. 'An overview of the historiography of women religious: a twenty-five year retrospective'. *US Catholic Historian*, 22:1, 1–26.

Coburn, C. K. and M. Smith. 1999. *How Nuns Shaped Catholic Culture and American Life, 1836–1920*. Chapel Hill and London: University of North Carolina Press.

Coleman, M. C. 1996. 'The symbiotic embrace: American Indians, white educators and the school, 1820s–1920s'. *History of Education*, 25:1, 1–18.

Collins, Jenny. 2015. 'They came with a Purpose: Educational Journeys of Nineteenth-century Irish Dominican Sister Teachers'. *History of Education*, 44:1, 44–63.

Collins, R. 1979. *The Credential Society: An Historical Sociology of Education and Stratification*. New York: Academic Press.

Conroy, J., Lundie, D., Davis, R., Baumfield, V., Barnes, L., Gallagher, T., Lowden, K., Bourque, N., and Wenell, K. 2013. *Does Religious Education Work? A Multi-disciplinary Investigation*. London: Bloomsbury.

Cooling, T. 2010. *Doing God in education*. London: Theos.

Copley, T. 2008. Non-Indoctrinatory Religious Education in Secular Cultures. *Religious Education*, 103:1, 22–31.

Cormier, A. 2018. Must schools teach religions neutrally? The Loyola case and the challenges of liberal neutrality in education. *Religion & Education*, 45:3, 308–330.

Cotter, C., and Robertson, D. 2016. "Introduction: The World Religions Paradigm in Contemporary Religious Studies". In Cotter, C. and Robertson, D. (eds.). *After World Religions: Reconstructing Religious Studies*. London and New York: Routledge. pp. 1–20.

Council of Europe. 2005. *The Religious Dimension of Intercultural Education (conference proceedings, Oslo, 2004)*. Council of Europe: Oslo.

Cox, J. L. 2007. *From Primitive to Indigenous*. Aldershot: Ashgate.

Crutchley, J., Parker, S. G., Roberts, S. (2019) *Sight, Sound and Text in the History of Education*. London: Routledge.

Cumming, A. 1985. 'Strife and dissension: missionary education in New Zealand, 1840–1853'. *Paedagogica Historica*, 25:2, 486–502.

Curthoys, A. and Lake, M. 2005. *Connected Worlds: History in Transnational Perspective*. Canberra: ANUE.

Curtis, S. 2000. *Educating the Faithful: Religion, Schooling and Society in Nineteenth-Century France*. DeKalb: Northern Illinois University Press.

Cush, D. 2018. Forty years of the British Journal of Religious Education and nearly fifty years' experience of non-confessional, multi-faith religious education: but are we any nearer agreeing the nature, scope and purpose of religious education in schools or achieving the necessary support to make it a success? *British Journal of Religious Education*, 40:1, 1–5.

Darian-Smith, K., Grimshaw, P. and Macintyre, S. 2007. *Britishness Abroad: Transnational Movements and Imperial Cultures*. Melbourne: Melbourne University Press.

David, M. 2016. "The Correspondence Theory of Truth". The Stanford Encyclopedia of Philosophy Retrieved 30th December 2018 <https://plato.stanford.edu/archives/ fall2016/entries/truth-correspondence/>.

Davis, A. 2010. Defending religious pluralism for religious education. *Ethics and Education*, 5:3, 189–202.

De Maeyer, J., Leplaae, S. and Schmiedl, J. eds. 2004. 'Religious Institutes in Western Europe in the 19th and 20th Centuries'. *Historiography, Research and Legal Position* (KADOC Studies on religions, Culture and Society, 2). Leuven: Leuven University Press.

Denzin, N. K. and Lincoln, Y. S. 2005. 'Introduction: The Discipline and Practice of Qualitative Research'. In Denzin, N. K. and Lincoln, Y. S. eds. *The Sage Handbook of Qualitative Research* 3rd edition. Thousand Oaks, CA: Sage.

De Vaulx, Bernard. 1961. *History of the Missions*. New York: Hawthorn Books.

Dewey, J. 1916 (1944). *Democracy and Education*. New York: The Free Press.

de Souza, M., Durka, G., Engebretson, K., Jackson, R., and McGrady, A., eds. 2006. *International Handbook of the Religious, Moral and Spiritual Dimensions in Education*. Dordrecht: Springer.

Dictionaries, O. Religion. Retrieved 30th December 2018 https://en.oxforddictionaries .com/definition/religion.

Donnelly, S. 2017. Understanding Childhood: child sex abuse and the Roman Catholic Church. In Strhan, A., Parker, S. G. and Ridgely, S. *The Bloomsbury Reader in Religion and Childhood*. London: Bloomsbury.

Dowd, B. and Tearle, S. eds. 1973. *Centenary History of the Presentation of the Blessed Virgin Mary, Wagga Wagga, New South Wales, 1874–1974*. Published by the Sisters of the PBVM: Wagga Wagga, NSW.

Doyle, Ann Margaret. 2017. 'Catholic Church and state relations in French education in the nineteenth century: the struggle between *laïcité* and religion'. *International Studies in Catholic Education*, 9:1, 108–122.

Dreeben, R. 1968. *On What is Learned in School*. Addison-Wesley Educational Publishers Inc.

Dries, A. 1998. *The Missionary Movement in American Catholic History*. New York: Orbis Books.

Durkheim, Émile. 1915 (1947). *The Elementary Forms of Religious Life*, translated by J. Swain. Glencoe, IL: Free Press.

Durkheim, E. 1926. *The elementary forms of the religious life. A study in religious sociology*. New York: Dover Publications.

Dworkin, G. A. et al: *The Sociology of Education* (January, 2013) at https://www .researchgate.net/publication/323953531_The_sociology_of_education.

Ebaugh, H. R. 1993. 'Patriarchal Bargains and Latent Avenues of Social Mobility: Nuns in the Roman Catholic Church'. *Gender and Society*, 7:3, 400–414.

Ebaugh, H. R. 2004. 'Religion Across Borders: Transnational Religious Ties.' *Asian Journal of Social Science*, 33:2, 216–231.

Elsdon-Baker, F. 2015. 'Creating creationists: The influence of 'issues framing' on our understanding of public perceptions of clash narratives between evolutionary science and belief.' *Public Understanding of Science*, 24.4, 422–439.

Encyclopaedia Britannica https://www.britannica.com/topic/sociology).

Engebretson, K., de Souza, M., Durka, G. and Gearon, L., eds. 2010. *International Handbook of Inter-religious Education*. Dordrecht: Springer.

Evans, S. 2008. 'The introduction of English-language education in early colonial Hong Kong'. *History of Education*, 37:3, 383–408.

Fitzgerald, T. 2003. 'Categories of friendship: mapping missionary women's educational networks in Aotearoa/New Zealand, 1823–40'. *History of Education*, 32:5, 513–527.

Fitzgerald, T. 2005. 'Archives of memory and memory of archive: CMS women's letters and diaries, 1823–35'. *History of Education*, 34:6, 657–674.

Forest, M. R. 2004. *With Hearts of Oak: The Story of the Sisters of the Presentation of the Blessed Virgin Mary in California, 1854–1907*. San Francisco: Sisters of the PBVM.

Fox, Noelle M. 2006. *An Acorn Grows among the Gums: The Presentation Sisters in Tasmania, 1866–2006*. Tasmania: Presentation Sisters Property Association.

Francis, M. and Dinham. A., 2016. *Religious Literacy in Policy and Practice*. Bristol: Policy Press.

Freathy, R., Parker, S., 2010. The necessity of historical inquiry in educational research: the case of religious education, *British Journal of Religious Education*, 32: 3, 229–243.

Freathy, R. J. K., Parker, S. G., Schweitzer, F., and Simojoki, H. (2014) 'Towards international comparative research on the professionalisation of Religious Education'. *Journal of Beliefs & Values: Studies in Religion & Education*, 35:2, 225–241.

Freathy, R., Parker, S. 2015. Prospects and problems for Religious Education in England, 1967–1970: curriculum reform in political context. *Journal of Beliefs and Values*, 36:1, 5–30.

Freathy, R., Doney, J., Freathy, G., Walshe, K., & Teece, G. (2017) 'Pedagogical Bricoleurs and Bricolage Researchers: The case of Religious Education'. *British Journal of Educational Studies*, 65:4, 425–443.

Fujivara, S. 2016. "Geertz vs Asad' in RE Textbooks: A Comparison Between England's and Indonesia's Textbooks'. In Berglund, J., Schanneik, Y., Bocking, B. *Religious Education in Global and Local World*. Switzerland: Springer.

Gadamer, H.-G., Weinsheimer, J., & Marshall, D. G. 2004. *Truth and method*. New York: Continuum.

Galvin, C. 1968. *From Acorn to Oak: A Study of Presentation Foundations, 1775–1968*. Fargo, North Dakota: Sisters of the PBVM.

Gardner, P. 1988. Religious Upbringing and the Liberal Ideal of Religious Autonomy. *Journal of Philosophy of Education*, 22:1, 89–105.

Gates, B. (ed). 2016. *Religion and Nationhood: insider and outsider perspectives on Religious Education in England.* Tubingen: Mohr Siebeck.

Garaty, Janice. 2013. *Providence Provides: Brigidine Sisters in the New South Wales Province.* Australia: University of New South Wales Press.

Garvey, B. 1994. 'Colonial schooling and missionary evangelism: the case of Roman Catholic educational initiatives in north-eastern Zambia, 1895–1953'. *History of Education*, 23:2, 195–206.

Gerdes, M. R. 1988. 'To educate and evangelize: black Catholic schools of the Oblate Sisters of Providence, 1828–1880', *US Catholic Historian*, 7:2, 183–199.

Gearon, L. 2013. MasterClass in religious education: transforming teaching and learning. London: Bloomsbury Academic.

Gearon, L. 2018. 'Paradigm shift in religious education: a reply to Jackson, or why religious education goes to war'. *Journal of Beliefs and Values.* 39:3, 358–378.

Gearon, L. and Prud'homme, J. 2018. *State Religious Education and the State of Religious Life.* Eugene: Pickwick.

Geaves, R. 2005. 'The dangers of essentialism: South Asian communities in Britain and the "world religions" approach to the study of religions'. *Contemporary South Asia* 14:1, 75–90.

Gervais, C. and Watson, A. 2014. 'Discipline, resistance, solace and the body: Catholic women religious' convent experience from the late 1930s to the late 1960s', *Religions* (March, 2014), 4. Downloaded 29 December 2018. https://www.mdpi .com/2077–1444/5/1/277/htm.

Geaves, R. 2005. 'The dangers of essentialism: South Asian communities in Britain and the "world religions" approach to the study of religions'. *Contemporary South Asia* 14:1, 75–90.

Grace, G. 2001. 'The state and Catholic schooling in England and Wales: Politics, Ideology and Mission Integrity'. *Oxford Review of Education*, 27: 4, 489–500.

Green, A. 1990. *Education and State formation: the Rise of Education Systems in England, France and the USA.* London: Macmillan.

Green, J. and Bloome, D. 1996. 'Ethnography and Ethnographers of and in Education'. In Heath, S.B., Flood, J. and Lapp, D. eds. *Handbook of Research on Teaching Literacy Through the Communicative and Visual arts.* New York and London: Macmillan Library Reference, 181–201.

Gresko, J. 2013. 'Mission and history: the Sisters of the Assumption and Japanese Students in Canada during World War II'. *Paedagogica Historica*, 49:4, 513–546.

Grimmitt, M. 2002. *Pedagogies of Religious Education: case studies in the research and development of good pedagogic practice in RE.* London: McCrimmon.

Grimmitt, M. 2010. *Religious Education and Social and Community Cohesion: an exploration of challenges and opportunities.* London: McCrimmon.

Gutmann, A. 1982. 'What's the use of going to school?'. In A. Sen & B. Williams. eds. *Utilitarianism and beyond*. Cambridge: Cambridge University Press, 261–277.

Habermas, J. 2015. *The Structural Transformation of the Public Sphere: an inquiry into a category of Bourgeois Society*. New York: Polity.

Hall, C. 2002. *Civilising Subjects: Colony and Metropole in the English Imagination*. Cambridge. Chicago: University of Chicago Press.

Hall, C. 2008. 'Making colonial subjects: education in the age of empire'. *History of Education*, 37: 6, 773–787.

Hand, M. 2003. 'A Philosophical Objection to Faith Schools'. *School Field*, 1:1, 89–99.

Hand, M. 2006. *Is religious education possible?: a philosophical investigation*. London/New York: Continuum.

Hand, M. 2008. What should we teach as controversial? A defense of the epistemic criterion. *Educational Theory*, 58:2, 213–228.

Hand, M. 2012. 'What's in a worldview? On Trevor Cooling's Doing God in education'. *Oxford Review of Education*, 38:5, 527–537.

Hand, M. 2015. Religious education and religious choice. *Journal of Beliefs and Values*, 36:1, 31–39.

Hand, M. 2018. *A theory of moral education*. New York: Routledge.

Hannam, P. 2019. *Religious Education and the Public Sphere*. Oxford: Routledge.

Haught, J. F. 1995. *Science and religion: from conflict to conversation*. New York: Paulist Press.

Hellinckx, B., Simon, F. and Depaepe, M. 2010. *The Forgotten Contribution of the Teaching Sisters: A Historiographical Essay on the Educational Work of Catholic Women Religious in the 19th and 20th Centuries*. Leuven: Leuven University Press.

Hewitt, G. 1977. *The Problems of Success: a History of the Church Missionary Society, 1910–1942*. London: SCM Press, 1971.

Hirst, P. H. 1974. *Knowledge and the curriculum: a collection of philosophical papers*. London: Routledge and Kegan Paul.

Holger, D. and Walford, G. 2004. *Educational Strategies Among Muslims in the Context of Globalization: Some National Case Studies*. Leiden: Brill.

Huel, R. 1996. *Proclaiming the Gospel to the Indians and the Métis: the missionary Oblates of Mary Immaculate in Western Canada, 1845 to 1945*. Alberta: University of Alberta Press.

Hull, J. 1982. ed. *New Directions in Religious Education* (New Directions Series). Lewes, Sussex: Falmer Press.

Hull, J. 1991. *God-Talk with Young Children*. London: Continuum.

Hull, J. 2014. *Towards the Prophetic Church*. London: SCM Press.

Huntington, S. P. 2002. *The clash of civilizations and the remaking of world order*. London: Simon and Schuster.

Hutch, W. 1875. *Nano Nagle: Her Life, Her Labours and Their Fruits.* Dublin: McGlashan and Gill.

Inoue, N. 2009. Religious Education in Contemporary Japan. *Religion Compass,* 3: 580–594.

International Knowledge Transfer in Religious Education—A Manifesto for Discussion: https://comenius.de/themen/Evangelische-Bildungsverantwortung-in-Europa/ 2019-Manifesto_on-International-Knowledge-Transfer-in-Religious-Education.pdf? m=1552893898.

Jackson, L. 2014. *Muslims and Islam in U.S. Education: Reconsidering multiculturalism.* London: Routledge.

Jackson, R. 1997. *Religious Education: An Interpretive Approach.* London: Hodder Education.

Jackson, R., Miedema, S., Weisse, W., & Willaime, J. P. eds. 2007. *Religion and educa- tion in Europe. Developments, contexts and debates.* Münster/New York/München/ Berlin: Waxmann.

Jackson, R. 2012. eds. *Religion, Education, Dialogue and Conflict. Perspectives on Reli- gious Education Research.* New York: Routledge.

Jackson, R. 2015. 'Misrepresenting religious education's past and present in looking for- ward: Gearon using Kuhn's concepts of paradigm, paradigm shift and incommensu- rability'. *Journal of Beliefs and Values,* 36:1, 64–78.

Jackson, R. 2018. 'Paradigm shift in religious education? A reply to Gearon, or when is a paradigm not a paradigm?'. *Journal of Beliefs and Values.* 39:3, 379–395.

Jackson, R. 2019. *Religious Education for Plural Societies.* Oxford: Routledge.

Jacomijn C. van der Kooij, Doret, de Ruyter, J. and Miedema, S. 2013. "Worldview": the Meaning of the Concept and the Impact on Religious Education, *Religious Education,* 108:2, 210–228.

Johnston, A. 2003. *Missionary Writing and Empire, 1800–1860.* Cambridge: Cambridge University Press.

Jonker, G. and Amiraux, V. 2006. *Politics of visibility: Young Muslims in European public spaces.* Bielefeld: De Gruyter.

Jordan, J. P. 1948. *Bishop Shanahan of Southern Nigeria.* Dublin: Clonmore and Reynolds.

Kallaway, P. 2009. 'Education, health and social welfare in the late colonial context: the International Mission Council and educational transition in the interwar years, with specific reference to colonial Africa'. *History of Education,* 38:2, 217–246.

Kant, I. 2003. *On Education.* New York: Dover Publications.

Kathan, B. W. 2013. 'Horace Bushnell and the Religious Education Movement'. *Religious Education: The official journal of the Religious Education Association,* 108:1, 41–57.

Kay, H. 2011. 'Being Muslim: Education and identities in late modern multicultural soci- eties'. *Discourse: Studies in the cultural politics of education.* 32:4, 475–479.

Kealy, M. 2007. *Dominican Education in Ireland, 1820–1930*. Dublin and Portland OR: Irish Academic Press.

Kilroy, P. 2000. *Madeleine Sophie Barat: a Life*. Cork: Cork University Press.

Kilroy, P. 2012. *The Society of the Sacred Heart in Nineteenth Century France*. Cork: Cork University Press.

Kittelmann-Flensner, K. 2015. *Religious Education in Contemporary Pluralistic Sweden*. Gothenburg: Gothenburg University Press.

Langmore, D. 1998. *Missionary Lives: Papua, 1874–1914*. Honolulu: University of Hawaii Press.

Leach, F. 2012. 'Resisting conformity: Anglican mission women and the schooling of girls in early nineteenth-century West Africa'. *History of Education*, 41:2, 133–153.

Leach, F. 2008. 'African girls, nineteenth-century mission education and the patriarchal imperative'. *Gender and Education*, 20:4, 335–347.

Labode, Modube. 1993. 'From Heathen Kraal to Christian Home: Anglican Mission Education and African Christian Girls, 1850–1900'. In Bowie, F., Kirkwood, D. and Ardener, S. *Women and Missions: Past and Present, Anthropological and Historical Perceptions*. Oxford and RI: Berg, 109–125.

Lee, L. 2017. *Recognizing the Non-Religious: reimagining the secular*. Oxford: OUP.

Lee, Y. 2013. 'Shikminji shigi Hoju seongyosa-eui gyoyukhwaldong: Hoju jangrohoe seongyobu jaryo-reul jungshim-euro.' [Trans: 'The Australian Presbyterian Mission in Colonial Korea'], *Hanguk Gyoyuksahak* [Trans: *Korean Journal of the History of Education*] 35:1, 265–91.

Lee, Y. 2016. 'Religion, modernity and politics: colonial education and the Australian mission in Korea, 1910–1941'. *Paedagogica Historica*, 52:6, 596–613.

Lei, C. 2000. 'The material culture of the Loretto School for girls in Hamilton, Ontario 1865–1971'. *Canadian Catholic Historical Association Historical Studies*, 66, 92–113.

Levinson, M. 1999. *The demands of liberal education*. Oxford: Oxford University Press.

Lewin, D. 2017a. *Educational philosophy for a post-secular age*. Abingdon/Oxford/New York: Routledge.

Lewin, D. 2017b. 'The hermeneutics of religious understanding in a postsecular age'. *Ethics and Education*, 12:1, 73–83.

Lewin, D. 2017c. 'Who's Afraid of Secularisation? Reframing the Debate Between Gearon and Jackson'. *British Journal of Educational Studies*, 65:4, 445–461.

Lewin, D. 2019. 'Towards a theory of pedagogical reduction: selection, simplification and generalisation in an age of critical education'. *Educational Theory*.

Lofland, J. 2006. *Analyzing Social Settings: A Guide to Qualitative Observation and Analysis* (4. ed.). Belmont, CA: Wadsworth.

Luddy, M. 2012. '"Possessed of Fine Properties": Power, Authority, and the Funding of Convents in Ireland, 1780–1900' in *The Economics of Providence*, edited by Maarten Van Dijck *et al*. Leuven: Leuven University Press.

Lundén, T. 2011 'Skolor som går over gränsen'. In Strandbrink, P., Lindqvist, B. and Forsberg, H. eds. *Tvära möten. Om utbildning och kritiskt lärande*. Stockholm/ Huddinge: Södertörn Studies in Education 1, 77–95.

Lynch, G. 2014. Saving the Child for the Sake of the Nation: moral framing and civic, moral and religious redemption of children. *American Journal of Cultural Sociology*. 2: 165–196.

MacCurtain, M. 1995. 'Late in the field: Catholic Sisters in twentieth century Ireland and the new religious history'. *Journal of Women's History*, 6:4 / 7:1, 49–63.

MacGinlay, M. R. 1996. *A Dynamic of Hope: Institutes of Women Religious in Australia*. Sydney: Crossing Press.

Magray, M. P. 1998. *The Transforming Power of the Nuns: Women, Religion and Cultural Change in Ireland, 1750–1900*. New York and Oxford: Oxford University Press.

Mangion, C. 2005. '"Good teacher" or "good religious"? the professional identity of Catholic women religious in nineteenth century England and Wales'. *Women's History Review*, 14:2, 223–42.

Mangion, C. 2008. *Contested Identities: Catholic Women Religious in Nineteenth-Century England and Wales*. Manchester: Manchester University Press.

Mason, A., and Wareham, R. 2018. 'Faith schools and civic virtue'. *Theory and Research in Education*, 16:2, 137–140.

Marples, R. 1978. 'Is Religious Education Possible? *Journal of Philosophy of Education*, 12:1, 81–91.

Marx, K. 1844. (1973). *Contribution to Critique of Hegel's Philosophy of Right*. Cambridge, England: Cambridge University Press.

Masuzawa, T. 2005. *The Invention of World Religions; or How European Universalism was Preserved in the Language of Pluralism*. Chicago, IL: University of Chicago Press.

Maussen, M., Vermeulen, F., Bader, V., and Merry, M. 2016. *Religious Schools in Europe: institutional opportunitities and contemporary challenges*. London: Routledge.

Mayrl, D. 2015. 'How does the State structure secularisation?'. *European Journal of Sociology*, 56:2, 207–239.

Mayrl, D. 2016. *Secular Conversions: political institutions and religious education in the United States and Australia, 1800–2000*. Cambridge: CUP.

McBride-Lindsey, R. 2017. *A Communion of Shadows: religion and photography in nineteenth-century America*. The University of North Carolina Press.

McGuinness, Margaret M. 2013. *Called to Serve: a History of Nuns in America*. New York and London: New York University Press.

McIntosh, E. 2015. Belonging without Believing, *International Journal of Public Theology*, 9:2, 131–155.

McLaughlin, T. B., Carr, D., Halstead, M., & Pring, R. 2008. *Liberalism, education and schooling: essays by T. H. McLaughlin*. Exeter: Imprint Academic.

Meijer, W., Miedema, S., and Lanser-van der Velde, A., eds. 2009. *Religious education in a world of religious diversity*. Münster/New York/München/Berlin: Waxmann.

Ment, D. M. 2011. 'The American role in education in the Middle East: ideology and experiment, 1920–1940'. *Paedagogica Historica*, 47:1–2, 173–189.

Melloni, A. and Caddedu, F. 2018. *Religious Literacy, Law and History: perspectives on European pluralist society*. London: Routledge.

Mercer, J. A. and Miller-McLemore, B., 2005. *Welcoming Children: a practical theology of childhood*. Atlanta: Chalice press.

Merry, M., Agirdag, O., & Driessen, G., 2017. 'The Catholic School Advantage and Common School Effect Examined: a comparison of Muslim immigrants and native pupils in Flanders.' *School Effectiveness and School Improvement* 28:1, 123–135.

Merry, M., 2018. 'Can Schools Fairly Select Their Students?'. *Theory and Research in Education* 16:3, 330–350.

Meyer, J. W. 1977. 'The Effects of Education as an Institution'. *American Journal of Sociology*, 83:1, 55–77.

Miedema, S. 2014. 'Coming out religiously! Religion, the public sphere and religious identity formation'. *Religious Education*, 109:4, 362–377.

Moles, A. 2015. 'Nudging for Liberals'. *Social Theory and Practice*, 41:4, 644–667.

Morgan, B., 2013. *On Becoming God: Late Medieval Mysticism and the Modern Self*, New York: Fordham University Press.

Morgan, D. (ed). 2009. *Religion and Material Culture: a matter of belief*. London: Routledge.

Morgan, D. 2012. *The Embodied Eye: religious visual culture and the social life of feeling*. Berkeley: University of California Press.

Morimoto, A. 2005. 'Understanding the People of Other Faiths: Conviviality Among Religions.' In Y. Murakami, N. Kawamura, & S. Chiba. eds. *Toward a Peaceable Future: Redefining Peace, Security, and Kyosei From a Multidisciplinary Perspective*. Seattle: Washington State University Press.

Morrison, H. 2011. '"Little vessels" or "little soldiers": New Zealand Protestant children, foreign missions, religious pedagogy and empire, c. 1880s–1930s'. *Paedagogica Historica*, 47:3, 303–321.

Morrison, H and Martin, M. C., 2017. *Creating Religious Childhoods in Anglo-World and British Colonial Contexts 1800–1950*. London: Routledge.

Murphy, D. 2000. *A History of Irish Emigrant and Missionary Education*. Dublin: Four Courts Press.

Murray, J. 2000. 'The Role of Women in the Church Missionary Society, 1799–1917'. In Ward, K. and Stanley, B. (eds). *The Church Mission Society and World Christianity, 1799–1992*. Grand Rapids and Richmond: William B. Eerdmans Publishing, 66–90.

Mustafa, H. 2014. 'Muslims in Copenhagen', *Tidskrift för islamforskning*. 8:1, 106–136.

Mwiria, K. 1991. 'Education for subordination: African education in colonial Kenya'. *History of Education*, 20:3, 261–273.

Nesbitt, E. M. 2004. *Intercultural Education: Ethnographic and Religious Approaches.* Brighton: Sussex Academic.

Nesbitt, E. 2011. 'The Teacher of Religion as Ethnographer'. In Clark, P. B. ed. *Oxford handbook of the sociology of religion.* Oxford: Oxford University Press.

Niehaus, I. 2011. 'Emancipation or Disengagement? Muslim Minorities and their Islamic Schools in Britain, the Netherlands and South Africa'. In Tayob, A., Niehaus, I. and Weisse, W. *Muslim Schools and Education in Europe and South Africa.* Münster: Waxmann.

Niell, S. 1964. *A History of Christian Missions.* London: Pelican Books.

Niell, S. 1985. *A History of Christianity in India, 1707–1858.* Cambridge: Cambridge University Press.

Niemi, K. .2015. 'Comparing Clementines and Satsumas: Looking at Religion in Indian Schools from a Nordic Perspective', *Religions of South Asia*, 9: 3, 332–355.

Noll, M. A., Bebbington, D. W., and Rawlyk, G. A. *Evangelicalism: Comparative Studies of Popular Protestantism in North America, the British Isles, and Beyond, 1700–1990.* New York and Oxford: Oxford University Press.

O'Connor, D. 1990. *Gospel, Raj and Sawarj: the Missionary Years of C. F. Andrews, 1904–14.* New York: Peter Lang.

O'Connor, D. 2000. *Three Centuries of Mission: the United Society for the Propagation of the Gospel, 1701–2000.* London: Continuum.

Oddie, J. 1999. *Missionaries, Rebellion and Proto-Nationalism: James Long of Bengal. 1814–87.* Surrey: Curzon Press.

O'Donoghue, T. 2001. *Upholding the Faith: the Process of Education in Catholic Schools in Australia, 1922–1965.* New York: Peter Lang.

Osmer, R. and Schweitzer, F. 2003. *Religious Education Between Modernization and Globalization: new perspective on the United States and Germany.* Cambridge: Eerdmans.

Ozgur, I., 2012. *Islamic Schools in Modern Turkey: Faith, Politics, and Education.* Cambridge: Cambridge University Press.

Owen, S. 2011. 'The World Religions Paradigm: Time for a Change'. *Arts & Humanities in Higher Education.* 10: 3, 253–268.

Parker, S., 2009. Theorizing sacred space in educational contexts: a case study of three English Midlands Sixth Form Colleges. *Journal of Beliefs and Values.* 30:1, 29–39.

Parker, S. 2017. Classrooms as spaces of religious and moral education and socialization. In Strhan, A., Parker, S. G. and Ridgely, S. *The Bloomsbury Reader in Religion and Childhood.* London: Bloomsbury.

Parker, S. G. 2012. Reinvigorating Christian Britain: the spiritual opportunities of the war, national identity, and the hope of Religious Education. In Parker, S. G. and

Lawson, T. (eds) *God and War: the Church of England and Armed Conflict in the Twentieth-century*. Aldershot: Ashgate.

Parker, S. G. and Freathy, R. 2012. 'Ethnic diversity, Christian hegemony and the emergence of multi-faith religious education in the 1970s', *History of Education: journal of the History of Education Society*, 41:3, 381–404.

Parker, S. G., Freathy, R. and Doney, J. 2016. 'The Professionalisation of Non-Denominational Religious Education in England: politics, organisation and knowledge'. *Journal of Beliefs and Values: studies in religion and education*, 37:2, 201–238.

Parker, S. G. and Freathy, R. 2020. The Church of England and Religious Education. In Rodgers, T. and Williamson, P. *The Church of England and British Political Culture in the Twentieth Century* Woodbridge: Boydell and Brewer.

Parker, S. G., Crutchley, J. and Roberts, S. 2020. *Religious Education: a broadcasting history*. Oxford: OUP.

Parsons, H. 1959. 'Reason, Affect and Value', *Educational Theory*, 9:2, 65–126.

Pearce, R. 1988. 'Missionary education in colonial Africa: the critique of Mary Kingsley', *History of Education*, 7: 4, 283–294.

Pels, T., & de Ruyter, D. J. 2011. 'The Influence of Education and Socialization on Radicalization: An Exploration of Theoretical Presumptions and Empirical Research'. *Child & youth care forum*, 41:3, 311–325.

Pirner, M., Lahnemann, J., Haussman, W., Schwarz, S., eds. 2018. *Public Theology, Religious Diversity, and Interreligious Learning*. London: Routledge.

Pirner, M., Lahnemann, J., Haussmann, W. and Schwarz, S. 2019. *Public Theology Perspectives on Religion and Education*. London: Routledge.

Polkinghorne, J. C. 1995. *Serious talk: science and religion in dialogue*. Valley Forge, Pa: Trinity Press International.

Pollefeyt, D., & Bouwens, J. 2014. *Identity in dialogue: Assessing and enhancing catholic school identity*. Zurich/Berlin: LIT-Verlag.

Porter, S. 2004. *Religion Versus Empire? British Protestant Missionaries and Overseas Expansion, 1700–1914*. Manchester and New York: Manchester University Press.

Porter, A., ed. 2003. *The Imperial Horizons of British Protestant Missions, 1880–1914*. Grand Rapids and Richmond: Eerdmans.

Pring, R. 2018. *The future of publicly funded faith schools: a critical perspective*. London: Routledge.

Prochner, L., May, H. and Kaur, B. 2009. '"The blessings of civilisation": nineteenth-century missionary infant schools for young native children in three colonial settings—India, Canada and New Zealand, 1820s–1840s'. *Paedagogica Historica*, 45:1–2, 83–102.

Ragsdale, John P. 1986. *Protestant Mission Education in Zambia, 1880–1954*. Associated University Press.

Raftery, D. 2012. 'Religions and the history of education: a historiography'. *History of Education*, 41:1, 41–56.

Raftery, D. 2013. *"Je suis d'aucune Nation"*: the recruitment and identity of Irish women religious in the international mission field, c. 1840–1940'. *Paedagogica Historica*, 49:4, 513–530.

Raftery, D. 2013. 'Rebels with a cause: obedience, resistance and convent life, 1800–1940'. *History of Education*, 42:6, 729–744.

Raftery, D. 2015. 'Teaching Sisters and transnational networks: recruitment and education expansion in the long nineteenth century'. *History of Education*, 44:6, 717–72.

Raftery, D. 2015. 'From Kerry to Katong: transnational influences in convent and novitiate life for the Sisters of the Infant Jesus, c. 1908–1950'. In Raftery, D. and Smyth, E. (eds). *Education, Identity and Women Religious, 1800–1900: Convents, Classrooms and Colleges*. Abingdon: Routledge.

Raftery, D. 2017. 'The Third Wave is Digital: Researching the History of Women Religious'. *American Catholic Studies*, 128: 2, 29–50.

Raftery, D. and Nowlan-Roebuck, C. 2007. 'Convent Schools and national Education in Nineteenth-Century Ireland: Negotiating a Place Within a Non-denominational System'. *History of Education*, 36: 3, 353–65.

Raftery, D. and Smyth, E. (eds 2015). *Education, Identity and Women Religious, 1800–1900: Convents, Classrooms and Colleges*. Abingdon: Routledge.

Rancière, J. 1991. *The ignorant schoolmaster: five lessons in intellectual emancipation*. Stanford, Calif: Stanford University Press.

Raughter, R. (ed). 2005. *Religious Women and their History*. Dublin: Irish Academic Press.

Rawls, J. 1996. *Political liberalism*. New York: Columbia University Press.

Religious Literacy Project. (ND). Retrieved from https://rlp.hds.harvard.edu/home.

Ricoeur, P., and Thompson, J. B. 1981. *Hermeneutics and the human sciences: essays on language, action and interpretation*. Cambridge: Cambridge University Press.

Ricoeur, P. 1995. *Figuring the Sacred: Religion, Narrative and the Imagination*, London: Fortress Press.

Ridgely, S. (ed) 2011. *The Study of Children in Religions: a methods handbook*. New York: New York University Press.

Riis, O. and Woodhead, L. (2012). *A Sociology of Religious Emotion*. Oxford: Oxford University Press.

Roebben, B. and Warren, R. (eds) 2001. *Religious Education as Practical Theology*. Leuven: Peeters.

Rogers, R. 2005. *From the Salon to the Schoolroom: Educating Bourgeois Girls in Nineteenth-Century France*. University Park: Pennsylvania State University Press.

Roger, R. 1998. 'Retrograde or Modern? Unveiling the Teaching Nun in Nineteenth-century France'. *Social History*, 23:2, 146–164.

Rooke, P. T. 1978. 'The pedagogy of conversion: missionary education to slaves in the British West Indies, 1800–1833'. *Paedagogica Historica*, 18:3, 356–374.

Rooke, P. T. 1980. 'Missionaries as pedagogues: a reconsideration of the significance of education for slaves and apprentices in the British West Indies, 1800–1838'. *History of Education*, 9:1, 65–79.

Rooke, P. T. 1994. 'Papists and proselytizers: non-denominational education in the British Caribbean after emancipation'. *History of Education*, 23:3, 257–273.

Ross, A. C. 2002. *David Livingstone: Mission and Empire*. London: Hambledon & London.

Russo, C. 2014. *International Perspectives on Education, Religion and Law*, London; Routledge.

Ryllis Clark, M. 2009. *Loreto in Australia*. Australia: University of New South Wales Press.

Said, E. W. 1978. *Orientalism: Western Conceptions of the Orient*. London: Penguin.

Scheer, M., Fadil, N. and Schepelern, J. (eds). 2018. *Secular Bodies, Affects and Emotions: european configurations*. London: Bloomsbury.

Schiffauer, W. & Baumann, G., Kastroyano, R., and Vertovec, S. ed. 2004. *Civil Enculturation: Nation State, School and Ethnic Difference in Four European Countries*. Oxford: Bergahn.

Schleiermacher, F. D. E. 2000. Texte zur Pädagogik: Kommentierte Studienausgabe: Band 2. Frankfurt: Suhrkamp.

Schleiermacher, F. D. E. 2011. *Brief Outline of Theology as a Field of Study: translation of the 1811 and 1830 editions (trans. Terrence. N. Tice)*. New York: Westminster/John Knox Press.

Schweitzer, F. and Boschki (eds). 2018. *Researching Religious Education: classroom processes and outcomes*. Munster: Waxmann.

Seton, R. 2013. *Western Daughters in Eastern Lands: British Missionary Women in Asia*. Santa Barbara, CA: Praeger.

Shillitoe, R. (Forthcoming 2020). *Negotiating Religion and Nonreligion in Childhood: Experiences of Worship in School*. London: Palgrave.

Shortt, J. 2018. 'Is Talk of 'Christian Education' Meaningful?'. In R. Stuart-Buttle and J. Shortt eds. *Christian Faith, Formation and Education*. New York: Palgrave Macmillan, 29–44.

Siegel, H. 2004. 'Faith, Knowledge and Indoctrination: A Friendly Response to Hand'. *School Field*, 2:1, 75–83.

Silver, H. 1992. 'Knowing and not knowing in the history of education'. *History of Education*, 21:1, 97–108.

Simmonds, S. 2014. Mapping the Curriculum-Making Landscape of Religion Education from a Human Rights Education Perspective. *Journal for the Study of Religion*, 27:1, 129–153.

Sjöborg, A. 2012. 'Aiming for the Stars? State Intensions for Religious Education in Sweden and Pupils' Attitudes'. In Jödicke, A. ed. *Religious Education Politics, the State, and Society*. Würzburg: Ergon Verlag.

Smart, N. 1996. *Dimensions of the sacred: an anatomy of the world's beliefs*. Berkeley, Calif/London: University of California Press.

Smart, N. 1998. *The World's Religions*. Cambridge: Cambridge University Press.

Smith, J. K. A. 2009. *Desiring the Kingdom: Worship, Worldview, and Cultural Formation*: Grand Rapids: Baker Academic.

Smith, W. C. 1998. *Faith and belief: the difference between them*. Oxford: Oneworld.

Stanford Encyclopedia of Philosophy: hhttps://plato.stanford.edu/entries/marx/.

Stanley, B. 1992. *The History of the Baptist Missionary Society, 1792–1992*. Edinburgh: T. and T. Clark.

Stanley, B. 2006. *Cambridge History of Christianity*. Cambridge: Cambridge University Press.

Strhan, A. Undated. Journal of Philosophy of Education. https://onlinelibrary.wiley .com/page/journal/14679752/homepage/education_and_the_problem_of_ religion.htm.

Strhan, A. Undated. 'Editorial: Education and the Problem of Religion' in Journal of Philosophy of Education virtual special issue: https://wol-prod-cdn.literatum online.com/pb-assets/assets/14679752/Religion_Editorial-1509467516000.pdf (accessed January 2019).

Strhan, A., Parker, S. G. and Ridgely, S. 2017. The Bloomsbury Reader in Religion and Childhood. London: Bloomsbury Press.

Smyth, B. T. 1994. *The Chinese Batch: the Maynooth Mission to China, 1911–1920*. Dublin: Four Courts Press.

Smyth, E. 1994. '"Much exertion of the voice, great application of the mind": Teacher Education within the Congregation of the Sisters of St Joseph of Toronto, 1854–1911'. *Canadian Catholic Historical Association Historical Studies*, 6:3, 97–113.

Smyth, E. (ed). 2007. *Changing Habits: Women's Religious Orders in Canada*. Toronto: Novalis.

Sociology of Education, Encyclopedia.com https://www.encyclopedia.com/social -sciences/encyclopedias-almanacs-transcripts-and-maps/sociology-education.

Suthren Hirst, J. and Zavos, J. 2005. 'Riding a tiger? South Asia and the problem of "religion"', *Contemporary South Asia*. 14: 1, 3–20.

Swartz, R. and Kallaway, P. 2018. 'Editorial: Imperial, global and local in histories of colonial education'. *History of Education*, 47:3, 362–367.

Takeshi, K. and Mangan, J. A. 1997. 'Japanese colonial education in Taiwan, 1895–1922: precepts and practices of control'. *History of Education*, 26:3, 307–322.

Tauft, A. and Broberg, M. 2018. 'Perspectives: Mediatized Religious Education'. In Lunby, K. ed. *Contesting Religion. The Media Dynamics of Cultural Conflicts in Scandinavia*. Berlin/Boston: DeGruyter.

Tauft, A. 2019. *Conflict and Entertainment, Media Influence on Religious Education in Upper Secondary School in Norway*. MF Norwegian School of Theology, Religion and Society. (In Press).

Tejirian, E. H. and Simon, R. S. eds. 2002. *Altruism and Imperialism: Western Cultural and Religious Missions in the Middle East.* New York: Middle East Institute, Columbia University.

Thaler R., and Sunstein, C., 2008. *Nudge: Improving Decisions about Health, Wealth, and Happiness.* Yale University Press.

Thiessen, E. J. 1993. *Teaching for commitment: liberal education, indoctrination, and Christian nurture.* Montreal; London: McGill-Queen's University Press, Gracewing.

Tillson, J. 2018. 'Rival conceptions of religious education'. In Paul Smeyers. ed. *International Handbook of Philosophy of Education* New York: Springer.

Tillson, J. 2019. *Children, Religion and the Ethics of Influence.* London: Bloomsbury.

Trimingham, J. C. 1998. 'Sacred symbols, school ideology and the construction of subjectivity'. *Paedagogica Historica*, 34:3, 771–94.

Trimingham, J. C. 2000. 'The lay sister in educational history and memory'. *History of Education*, 29:3, 181–194.

Ulich, R. 1968. *A History of Religious Education: documents and interpretations from the Judaeo-Christian tradition.* New York: New York University Press.

Underwood, L. 2014. *Childhood, Youth and Religious Dissent in Post-Reformation England.* London: Palgrave.

Vallgårda, K., 2015. *Imperial Childhoods and Christian Mission: education and emotions in South India and Denmark.* London: Palgrave.

Van der Walt, Johannes L. 2011. 'Religion in education in South Africa: was social justice served?'. *South African Journal of Education*, 31:3, 381–393.

Van Manen, M. 1991. *The tact of teaching: the meaning of pedagogical thoughtfulness.* Albany: State University of New York Press.

Vanderstraeten, R. 2014. 'Religious activism in a secular world: the rise and fall of the teaching congregations of the Catholic Church'. *Paedagogica Historica*, 50:4, 494–513.

Voice, P. 2014. 'Comprehensive doctrine'. In J. Mandle and Reidy, D. eds. *The Cambridge Rawls Lexicon.* Cambridge: Cambridge University Press, 126–129.

Wainwright, W. J. 2005. *The Oxford handbook of philosophy of religion.* Oxford: Oxford University Press.

Walsh, O. 1995. 'The Dublin University Mission Society, 1890–1905', *History of Education*, 24:1, 61–72.

Ward, K. and Stanley, B. eds. 2000. *The Church Mission Society and World Christianity, 1799–1999.* Grand Rapids and Richmond: Eerdmans.

Wareham, R. 2017. Faith Schools, Indoctrination and Non-exclusivist Religious Claims Retrieved from https://blogs.warwick.ac.uk/faithschooling/entry/faith_schools_indoctrination/.

Walford, G. 2007. *Methodological developments in ethnography.* Amsterdam & Oxford: Elsevier JAI.

Warner, M., VanAntwerpen, J., & Calhoun, C. J. 2010. Varieties of secularism in a secular age. Cambridge, Mass: Harvard University Press.

Watts, R. 1998. *Gender, Power and the Unitarians in England, 1760–1860.* London: Longman.

Watts, R. 2009. 'Education, empire and social change in nineteenth century England'. *Paedagogica Historica,* 45:6, 773–786.

Weber, M. 1958. (1905) *The Protestant Ethic and the Spirit of Capitalism, translated by Talcott parsons.* New York: Charles Scribner and Sons.

Weisse, W. (2010) REDCo: A European Research Project on Religion in Education. *Religion & Education.* 37 (3), 187–202.

Weisse, W. 2013. 'Dialogical 'Religious Education for all' in Hamburg'. *Pedagogiek* 33, 166–178.

Whitehead, C. 1995. 'The medium of instruction in British Colonial education: a case of cultural imperialism or enlightened paternalism?'. *History of Education,* 24:1, 1–15.

Whitehead, C. 2003. *Colonial Educators.* London: IB Tauris.

Whitehead, C. 1999. 'The Contribution of the Christian Missions to British Colonial Education'. *Paedagogica Historica,* 35:1, 321–337.

Whitehead, C. 2005. 'The historiography of British imperial education policy, Part I'. *History of Education,* 34:4, 441–454.

Whitehead, C. 'The historiography of British imperial education policy, Part II: Africa and the rest of the colonial empire'. *History of Education,* 34:4, 441–54.

Wright, A. 2004. *Religion, education, and post-modernity.* London/New York: Routledge Falmer.

Wright, A. 2006. 'Research in Religious Education: Philosophical and Theological Perspectives.' *Religious Education,* 101:2, 175–178.

Yap, Dilys. 2001. *The Convent Light Street: a History of a Community, a School and a Way of Life.* Penang: Phoenix.

Zaman, M., & Memon, N., 2016. *Philosophies of Islamic Education: Historical Perspectives and Emerging Discourses.* London: Routledge.

List of English Language Journals in R&E and Their Websites

British Journal of Religious Education https://www.tandfonline.com/loi/cbre20

Christian Education Journal https://us.sagepub.com/en-us/nam/christian-education -journal/journal203471#description

Christian Higher Education https://www.tandfonline.com/action/journalInformation ?show=aimsScope&journalCode=uche20

Greek Journal of Religious Education http://www.gjre.gr/en/

International Journal of Children's Spirituality https://www.tandfonline.com/loi/ cijc20

International Journal of Education and Religion https://brill.com/view/journals/ijer/ ijer-overview.xml

International Journal of Christianity and Education https://journals.sagepub.com/ home/ice

Journal of Beliefs and Values https://www.tandfonline.com/loi/cjbv20

Journal of Childhood and Religion http://childhoodandreligion.com/

Journal of Christianity and Higher Education http://ojs.umobile.edu/index.php/TBD

Journal of Religious Education https://link.springer.com/journal/40839

Journal of Research on Christian Education https://www.tandfonline.com/action/jour nalInformation?show=aimsScope&journalCode=urce20

Religion and Education https://www.tandfonline.com/loi/urel20

Religious Education https://www.tandfonline.com/loi/urea20